THE
CHECKLIST

INDIE PUBLISHING MY WAY

MARSHA WARD

Titles by Marsha Ward

Fiction:

Gone for a Soldier
The Man from Shenandoah
Spinster's Folly
Ride to Raton
Trail of Storms

The Zion Trail

Blood at Haught Springs
Faith and the Foreman

Nonfiction:

Rapid Recipes for Writers... and Other Busy People
From Julia's Kitchen: Owen Family Cookery

Simple Book List and Purchase Links

marshaward.com/bookshelf/simple-list

THE CHECKLIST

INDIE PUBLISHING MY WAY

MARSHA WARD

WestWard Books
ক ♦ ক
Payson, Arizona

WestWard Books
P O Box 53
Payson, Arizona 85547

Table of Contents

Why This Book Can Help You

I've been writing for over thirty years. For much of that time, I've published my work: books, stories, "chapbooks," newsletters, and small press publications, by myself—or independently. I was an Indie Author and Publisher before it was "cool." Way before the Indie Revolution.

Because of my background, hardly a week goes by that someone doesn't contact me to pick my brain about writing or indie publishing. However, email messages, phone calls, and Facebook Messenger chats are not optimal communication vehicles for imparting this kind of knowledge. Merely answering the questions uppermost in a person's mind when they sought me out could not begin to impart the world of information that I've learned about writing and self- or indie-publishing. I often thought it would take a book to tackle the mountain of stuff to know so a prospective writer could begin their publishing path effectively.

So I wrote the book.

The Checklist: Indie Publishing My Way, is designed to help aspiring and experienced writers new to the indie publishing world get their work before the reading public in an organized manner, without missing crucial steps. This book introduces those new to this experience The Checklist I use for publishing books My Way, plus a few vital steps beyond those I use in my established process (because I take short cuts, based on my knowledge). Note that I use this Checklist for regular releases, not pre-orders.

You'll see that I publish an electronic or ebook first. Why? I want to make the book available to those who read ebooks as soon as possible. This is due to simple economics. I sell many more ebooks than print books, so getting the ebook uploaded and out to market is good for my bottom line. Another reason is that formatting for print is more time-intensive for me, so I save that task for after I have written the work and released it as an ebook. I will eventually do a print version of each work, but it will happen after I release the ebook.

It doesn't matter to me whether the piece I work on is long or short, or if it's fiction or nonfiction. The process is pretty much the same for any book I publish. Bear in mind that this is what *I* do, what *my* checklist is, for publishing books. I'll give you the checklist, divided into processes, then I'll expand on each section in a chapter in this book. You won't need to take notes while you read the Checklist. I go into detail in the sections pertaining to each step. I'll also cover the unfamiliar words and processes along the way.

Enjoy!
Marsha Ward
May 3, 2017

A Note on Organizing Your Computer Folders

I sometimes see anguished messages that a writer has lost an important file containing precious creative work somewhere on their computer. This is a heart-wrenching situation. Most of the time, someone reminds them that they can find it again by initiating a search with that function of their computer's operating system (OS). However, there's an almost-foolproof way of not losing the file in the bowels of their computer in the first place. Put it in its own folder.

Whether a computer is a PC or a Mac, it has a folder organization hierarchy, beginning with Documents, My Documents, or something of the sort. I'm a PC girl, so I'll use the jargon I'm most familiar with in this advice.

The first thing I do when I set up a new computer is see if there is a "My Data" folder under "My Documents." If not, I add a My Data folder to the My Documents folder. It's going to be the most-used folder on my computer. Inside that goes a "My Writing" folder. Each project I write has its own folder therein, usually within a sub-folder for the kind of writing it is, that is, Novels, Novellas, Short Stories, Collections, Nonfiction, and so on.

If your body of work isn't yet extensive, you might skip the Genre Folder step and rely on recognizing your Titles. Do go ahead and make sure you have a readily apparent place in which to save your manuscript so you won't suffer the anguish of losing your work because you don't know where it got saved.

Just as you will write your work in your own way, you have my permission to organize your folders according to your own preferences. I don't care if you open a designated project folder on your desktop. Do make sure you have one place for that project, so your files aren't scattered hither and yon and in danger of getting lost. However it is that you organize your file folders, you can still use *The Checklist*.

Remember: always, always back up that precious work to another safe location or two, whether that is a flash drive or two, an external drive, or a backup service on the Cloud.

The Checklist

1 - FIRST DRAFT

1. Write the book.
2. Assemble and keep track of your team.
3. Download free software.
4. Set up an Internet Presence.
5. Open an account with an email service provider.
6. Decide how you want to distribute your book.
7. Download the free Smashwords Style Guide.
8. If you plan to have a print edition of your book, open an account at CreateSpace.
9. If you plan for a print edition, decide on the trim size (dimensions) of your book.
10. Start the ebook Cover Design process.
11. If you will do a print edition, start the Print Cover Design process at the same time.
12. Contract with an editor.
13. Finish the First Draft.

2 - SECOND DRAFT

1. Check for misspellings and other boo-boos.
2. Make a copy of the Second Draft for Beta Readers.
3. Send Manuscript to Beta Readers.
4. Set release dates for ebook and print editions.
5. Decide on prices for ebook and print editions.
6. Make decisions on business set-up.
7. Start mentioning your book.
8. Get Beta Reader comments back.

3 - THIRD DRAFT

1. Incorporate changes from Beta Readers.
2. Decide if you will use book sales tracking sites.

4 - FOURTH DRAFT

1. Clean up your punctuation and spacing.
2. Have a professional author photo taken.
3. Get informed about Authorgraph.

5 - SEND TO EDITOR

1. Send your polished manuscript to your editor.
2. Get the edited manuscript back.

6 - FIFTH DRAFT

1. Print out the manuscript to read aloud.
2. Make corrections to your manuscript file and rename it.
3. Add Front Matter to the file.

7 - FOLDERS, FILES, AND ENDORSERS

1. Figure out folder structure.
2. Final Book Block File Copies.
3. Edit EBook File to avoid odd formatting (optional).
4. Create Folders as Needed.
5. Make Copyright Registration File (optional).
6. Prepare Other Formats for Endorsers.
7. Send File to Endorsers.

8 - EBOOK COVER

1. Check and Complete Requirements for EBook Cover.

9 - PREPARE FOR EBOOK FORMATTING

1. Create Standard EBook Configuration
2. Copy the EBook Final Book Block file.
3. Add Front and Back Matter.
4. Create and Apply Styles.

10 - EBOOK FORMATTING

1. Discover Specifications for Vendors.
2. Read the Smashwords Style Guide.
3. Contract with a Formatter.
4. Make Copies and Format.

11 - ADVANCE READER COPIES

1. Make eARC Copy.
2. Create eARCs for Reviewers and Bloggers.
3. Send eARCs.

12 - PREPARE FOR UPLOADING

1. Receive all endorsements.
2. Create book description(s).
3. Determine categories and keywords.
4. ISBNs

13 - PRINT BOOK FORMATTING

1. Assemble the Parts.
2. Templates and Guides.
3. Contract with a Formatter.
4. Review the CreateSpace Process.
5. Format the Print Interior file.
6. Save the finished file.
7. Save the Print final as a pdf file.

14 - PRINT COVER

1. Create the Back Cover Information for Your Print Book.
2. Create the Full Book Cover.

15 - PRINT BOOK SETUP

1. Start print setup at CreateSpace.
2. Be consistent with subtitles or series titles.
3. Designate an ISBN for your book.
4. Choose the physical properties for your book.
5. Check that you are on target for your Print edition release date.

16 - CREATE A BUZZ FOR YOUR BOOK

1. Prior to release, send out your newsletter.
2. Alert your team that your ebook release is approaching.
3. Make use of all your social media sites to announce your forthcoming book.

17 - UPLOAD EBOOKS PRIOR TO RELEASE DAY

1. Upload ebook files to each online vendor.
2. If you use Smashwords as a distributor, download ePub and mobi files.
3. Check the files on your computer.
4. Create an Author Central account at Amazon.
5. Collect purchase links in a spreadsheet.
6. Update your sites.
7. Add your book to online book catalogs.

18 - EBOOK RELEASE DAY

1. Announce your ebook on the designated release day.
2. Register the ebook ISBN with Bowker.
3. Register the copyright to your ebook.
4. Update your websites again.
5. Submit materials to online publicity sites of published books.
6. Inform your writers' organizations.
7. Open an account at Authorgraph and add your ebook.
8. Open accounts of your choice for book sales tracking.
9. Carry out marketing efforts of your choice.

19 - FOUR TO SIX WEEKS BEFORE PRINT BOOK RELEASE DAY

1. Gather print interior and book cover files.
2. Upload both print book pdf and cover pdf to CreateSpace.
3. Finish Setup at CreateSpace.
4. Check your book for visual errors.
5. Allow up to two weeks for proof to arrive.

6. Check the print proof copy.
7. Approve the proof. Publish your book.
8. Order print book copies.
9. Wait for copies to arrive.
10. Claim print book at Author Central when it appears.
11. Make sure ebook and print book are linked on Amazon.

20 - PRINT BOOK RELEASE DAY

1. Announce the print book launch on the designated day.
2. Add the print edition to GoodReads.
3. Register the print ISBN with Bowker.
4. Carry out the marketing efforts of your choice.

Chapter 1
FIRST DRAFT

1. Write the Book.

The essential step in publishing a book is writing it. Yeah. That. This step will take however long it does, but the sooner you develop habits that help you move forward—without an internal editor on your shoulder to make you write, rewrite, polish, and re-polish Chapter 1—the better. It doesn't matter whether or not you own the most popular writer's software out there, or if you write your 1st draft using Word, Open Office, Pages, or Notepad. The point is to push through and finish the draft, because you can't publish a book that isn't finished.

On my checklist, I allow two to three months for writing. Sometimes I hit it, and sometimes I don't, Because Life. Happens. Did I mention that I have a condition known as ADHD? That's Attention Deficit Hyperactivity Disorder. A great many creative people—or Creatives, for short—suffer from this malady in its various forms. The condition is difficult to deal with, but all challenges can be overcome (or so I keep telling myself).

Here's a Truth that you must remember: every writer writes differently. In other words, there is no One True Way to write. Don't let anyone fool you into thinking that *their* method for writing is the *only* method of writing.

The corollary to the Truth is that every writer may write each book differently. Okay, I don't want to scare you or introduce unneeded stress into your life, so I won't say much more about that. Just realize that you may need to write a second book using a different method. No stressing about it, okay? Just get this book finished.

Writers write using methods that string along a spectrum that ranges from Plotter at one end to Pantser at the other. Where you may fall on this spectrum (and it probably will shift from time to time and book to book) depends on how your brain is wired. Plotters feel a compulsion to know everything that will happen in a book, so they plot it out, using outlines of varying degrees of exactitude and comprehensiveness. Pantsers (the name comes from the term "writing-by-the-seat-of-your-pants") are also called organic or discovery writers. They want to write the story and discover what happens as their fingers work on the keyboard. You'd be surprised how many top authors are Pantsers. Really surprised.

Pantsers often are stymied by complete outlines. For example, if I write so little as a synopsis of a book, my brain says, "Well, look there, you've written the story. You don't need me anymore," and it shuts down and refuses to cooperate with me in writing a first draft.

There is so much danger in this state of affairs that I cannot plot out a book. I can only figure out who the main character is, a vague estimate of where the book could end, and maybe a couple or three things I hope will happen along the way. I usually know when and where the story will be set, and maybe what the "inciting incident" or "change in the character's life" is. Beyond that, I have to let my mind direct my fingers when I write.

The process is really kind of cool.

That doesn't mean it's *your* process. It's mine. And it can change. Slightly.

Different books I've written have called for different degrees of foreknowledge, so I have ranged a bit from the Pantser end toward the Plotter end, but never so much that my brain turned off.

Go with what works for you in writing your book, but do go forward.

2. Assemble and Keep Track of Your Team

While you write the Book, set up a paper or electronic spreadsheet for noting information about the persons you will need to recruit for your Support Team.

As you are writing your book, you'll have downtime. In these periods, there are several things you really should do to advance your project. This includes recruiting and keeping track of the people you need on your Support Team to make your book project a success.

For easy tracking, set up your Support Team Spreadsheet. It doesn't matter if it's a paper spreadsheet or an electronic one like in Excel or OpenOffice. The important thing is keeping it updated as you add people and what they agree to do for you.

You need to spend time recruiting all the vital people you need to help you build buzz for your book. You'll find them as you interact with people, usually on social media, but some you might find in your actual life.

Recruit these folks right now and from now on: Beta Readers, Endorsers, Bloggers, Reviewers, and Friends and Fans who agree to publicize your book around release day. Be sure to get their email addresses and find out what file format of your manuscript (MS, for short) they prefer to receive from you. Note these items in your spreadsheet. Save it in your physical or electronic book Folder.

Beta Readers. You need people to read and comment on your first draft. These are called Beta Readers. Pick trustworthy people that you know have skills in grammar, or can spot plot holes. Get a couple to read for enjoyment and report back where the story lagged or they lost interest. This is important to know! Most writers use from three to seven beta readers. Be sure to give each one instructions on what feedback you want from them, and give them a deadline you both can work with when you send them your First Draft file. Be aware that you might catch the people you've signed up as beta readers at a bad time when you've actually finished your draft, so having a large group of beta readers from which to choose is good.

So, who is the Alpha Reader? You are, although if you work with a critique partner or group, they might also be called alpha readers. Think of the alpha reader as the one with "first eyes on the work."

Endorsers. You might know writers of some measure of celebrity, or experts in the topic you are writing about, that you could ask to read your book and give their endorsement of it. This is becoming less important in the digital age, though. If you can't find anybody to endorse the book, don't stress about it.

Bloggers and Reviewers. If you know any bloggers who review books of your genre, this is the time to enlist their help for creating buzz about your book around the time of the release date. Offer to write guest blogs, give them a pre-made interview, or promise them the following materials when the time comes for them to boost your book: book details (title, author, publisher, genre, release date), cover image, excerpts, endorsements, purchase links, author bio, and the like. You could also ask for them to participate in a cover reveal prior to the book's release. Enlist the aid of Fans or Friends who are likely to read your book to write and post reviews to Amazon and GoodReads when the time comes. Talk to your contacts on Facebook, LinkedIn, or other social media, to ask them to mention your book. All of this creates buzz building up to release day.

Fans and Friends. You might have friends who are excited about the fact that you are writing a book. If this is not your first book, you might have fans who like your work. Enlist their help in creating a buzz about your book, especially in the last few weeks before its release. Encourage them to talk up your book on their social media accounts, and to their friends who might enjoy your new book.

There are other vital members of your support team, which we'll address later in this chapter. Make sure to put them on the spreadsheet, too. Keep track of dates and deadlines with them, as well.

3. Download free software.

The Internet teems with free software, and when you're indie publishing, here are three that are extremely useful, and one other that I use.

Calibre. This software program is known partly as a library manager for your ebooks, but it also is the conversion tool I use for making ePub and mobi files to send to various people on my team. This is accomplished by doing a "Save-As" of the file I need to convert in Calibre, and saving it as "Web Page, filtered." This creates an .htm file. Then I open Calibre, click the Add books icon, upload the .htm file to Calibre, add metadata, and then convert to the file formats I need.

Download it and get to know it through the online help files.

https://calibre-ebook.com/

Adobe Digital Editions. This is an ereader for ePub files, and is useful for checking them when you use Smashwords's MeatGrinder conversion tool or generate them yourself (More on Smashwords later). Download it from

http://www.adobe.com/solutions/ebook/digital-editions/download.html.

Kindle Previewer. This tool shows you how your Kindle mobi file will appear on various Kindle devices. You'll use it after you upload your file to the Kindle Direct Publishing site. Just afterward, you'll download the processed file to test with Kindle Previewer. Download this free software from

https://www.amazon.com/gp/feature.html?docId=1000765261.

yWriter5 & 6. Since the software I use to write my manuscripts is free, I'll mention it. This Windows and Linux writing software is the creation of Australian author Simon Haynes, whose day job is software programmer. Handy, huh? When he couldn't find a writer's software that suited him, he made his own, and provides it free-of-charge to other writers throughout the world. yWriter has many useful functions for authors. It breaks writing down to the scene level, then chapters in the manuscript. It has the capacity to create character lists, locations, items, timelines, and many more neat things, including exporting manuscripts as ebooks (which I don't yet use). yWriter has been around for several years. There are two versions on offer currently. yWriter5, which I use, has been the standard issue for several years, but Simon has updated it for version 6.0.0.0, more suitable for Windows computers running Win 8 operating system and above. Download either version from

http://spacejock.com.

4. Set up an Internet Presence.

I'm going to urge you to have some kind of Internet presence that is your own, such as a website, or at the very least, a blog. Being visible on the Internet is a given if you plan to be a writer. It's best to own a domain name related to the name you write under (okay, you really pay rent on it for a specified time period. Get two years to begin.). Unless you're an Internet and computer wizard, you also need to have or rent space for your site somewhere, possibly from a hosting company. And you need to build the site itself, or pay someone to create it for you. But there are plenty of themes—that is, pre-coded arrangements for website—available for crafting a site on a variety of content management platforms. Use Google and YouTube as resources, because the options are endless, and only you know what you want. And if you don't know, go look at the sites of authors you know. Also, ask your author friends what kind of set-ups they like best. If you don't have any author friends, it's time you got connected. Seek out helpful author communities on Facebook, for example. Ask in your local library if there are groups meeting in your location.

My website is at http://marshaward.com.

5. Open an account with an email service provider.

Most publishing advice books tell writers that they cannot do without an emailed newsletter sent to subscribers for contact, engagement, and marketing purposes. Here are a few email service or marketing providers that offer free plans to get you started when you have fewer numbers of subscribers.

MailChimp https://mailchimp.com/
MadMimi https://madmimi.com/
MailerLite https://www.mailerlite.com/

I use MailChimp. Some of my friends use the other two services or others. Set up your account somewhere now and set about getting people to subscribe with signup forms you can place on your blog or website and social media sites. When you have a few subscribers, start reaching out and making them dedicated fans by sending them newsletters about yourself and your life as a writer, whether you be at the beginner level or established.

6. Decide how you want to distribute your book.

You have at least two choices in the types of books available in the world. There are more, but let's start with print books and electronic or ebooks, These are the two distribution choices you want to consider first.

I believe every person who thinks about writing a book "sees it" on a brick-and-mortar bookstore shelf. Here are two realities: there are few brick-and-mortar bookstores anymore, and it's nearly impossible to get independently published books on bookstore shelves. I know it's hard to let go of that dream, but don't hit your head against a brick-and-mortar stone wall unnecessarily.

My reality is that I sell many more ebooks than print books. I maximize my profits by aiming principally at the ebook market. However, many people still prefer print books, so I do create and publish a print edition of my works. I use these for hand-selling to local fans or for selling at events. The print editions of my works are also sold on the Amazon website, the Barnes and Noble website, and at a few other sites, so readers *can* find them if they prefer print.

Some authors have their ebooks uploaded only to Amazon through the Kindle Direct Publishing website, or in the KDP Select program, which demands exclusivity. Since my philosophy (and the best business advice I've come across) is not to put all my eggs in one basket, but to seek out multiple revenue streams, I distribute my ebooks widely, that is, not just with the KDP Select program. There are authors who have other distribution plans, but this is how I do it My Way.

My ebooks are available on Amazon as Kindle ebooks, but also are available on Barnes and Noble's website for NOOK books, on Kobo Books, on iTunes, and on many other vendors worldwide.

I could have opened accounts to upload directly to the major vendors, but I chose to use a site called Smashwords.com (https://www.smashwords.com/) as my distributor. Their MeatGrinder conversion software creates all the files needed for distribution to their retail partners. In addition, I upload directly to Amazon's Kindle Direct Publishing (KDP) program, but I do *not* opt into the Select program.

Although there are advantages of quicker reporting and sometimes more frequent payments through direct uploading to some sites, I choose to save the time that preparing files, uploading them, and monitoring the sites would take by using Smashwords. There is no upfront cost. All the ebook publishing programs I have listed here make their money from taking a percentage from sales made.

Once you've decided how you're going to distribute, open upload accounts with your chosen vendors, whether it be only

KDP https://kdp.amazon.com/

or at the other major ebook publishing platforms like

nookpress https://www.nookpress.com/ebooks,
Kobo Writing Life https://www.kobo.com/writinglife,

or using Apple's iBooks Author app
http://www.apple.com/ibooks-author/.

You may need a Mac computer to use that and I don't have one, which is why I go through Smashwords. If you're like me and don't have time to deal with multiple sites, you may choose as your wide distributor

Smashwords (https://www.smashwords.com/), or Draft 2 Digital, another ebook distributor (https://www.draft2digital.com/).

There's nothing to keep you from using both, so long as you sort out which partners you wish them to send your files to, that is, don't opt in to Barnes and Noble at both distributors.

7. Download the free Smashwords Style Guide.

Smashwords has an excellent, free Style Guide for formatting ebooks. Even if you decide not to use Smashwords as a distributor, do set up an account so you can download the Style Guide and other ebooks at Smashwords. In addition to free ebooks from various authors, they have two notable sales during the year. One is typically the first week of March, which is "Read an Ebook Week," and the other occurs during the entire month of July, their Summer/Winter Sale (counting both hemispheres of the earth). I use the coupon feature from time to time to reward faithful readers and mailing list subscribers with discounts up to 100% off (you know, FREE).

Download the Smashwords Style Guide here: https://www.smashwords.com/books/view/52.

Smashwords offers other free guides, such as the Book Marketing Guide found here: https://www.smashwords.com/books/view/305.

8. If you plan to have a print edition of your book, open an account at CreateSpace.

I use CreateSpace.com to print and distribute my print books. If you plan on creating a print edition of your book, open an account at

https://www.createspace.com/.

There are other options for independent authors to get print books made, but competitive pricing for author copies and exemplary customer service keep me at CreateSpace.

CreateSpace has templates to download to assist you in formatting your print books. Many websites offer advice on how to format print books by yourself. I cover more about print book creation in Chapters 13, 15, and 19.

9. If you plan for a print edition, decide on the trim size (dimensions) of your book.

For now, you need to know that the earlier you decide on the trim size, or dimensions, of your print book, the better. Standard sizes for novels are 5 inches by 8 inches (expressed as 5x8), 5.25x8, 5.5x8.5, and 6x9. Measure the books in your bookcase to see what those sizes actually look like, and determine which size you like best. One guideline you might consider is to use a smaller trim size if your book will have few pages. This will make it thicker, rather than thin and floppy.

CAUTIONS:

One: I *highly* recommend that you do NOT use the print book option at nook press. The program is supplied by a well-known vanity outfit that I *strongly do not recommend.* Use CreateSpace instead.

Two: I also do not recommend that you use the ebook creation option from CreateSpace, nor the print book option from KDP. While you are not at risk in your pocketbook like you would be using nook press's print option, the results of taking the short cuts are not optimal. At this time, KDP's print option doesn't allow for proof copies or author copies, and CreateSpace's Kindle option doesn't make good ebooks.

10. Start the ebook Cover Design process.

As you work on your First Draft, spend time looking at covers from traditional authors writing in your genre. Search on Amazon to see book covers in the mystery, thriller, suspense, western, romance, or whatever genre you are writing. Notice the colors used, the fonts, the placement of the type. Realize that book covers don't illustrate scenes or characters from your book. They create an atmosphere, and scream to the reader: "This is a mystery/romance/action adventure." Not *all* of those. Your genre.

Once you've identified how your cover should look for your genre, it is time to decide where to get your ebook/print cover. Unless you are a graphic designer skilled in the creation of book covers, it's best to seek out a professional cover designer to make your book cover. After all, the cover is what a reader sees first. *You never get a second chance to make a first impression!*

Many cover designers offer premade covers specifically for ebooks on their sites. Use a search engine with the term "premade book covers" to discover them. Also, look at sites that sell premade covers from many designers, such as SelfPubBookCovers

https://www.selfpubbookcovers.com/.

Premades typically cost far less than custom designed covers. I've found and purchased several premade covers that fit current or future projects to a T. Do find out how much revision the designer will do to the premade. Will they change out the font for another, change the placement of the font, swap out images?

Whether you select a premade cover or contract for a custom cover design, make sure the designer will furnish a high-resolution (hi-res) jpg file of the ebook cover. You will want one to include in or with the completed manuscript you send to your reviewers and bloggers.

If you're brave enough to make your own ebook cover, these videos from Derek Murphy may be of assistance:

How to make an ebook cover in Microsoft Word (Part 1)
https://www.youtube.com/watch?v=h_6zDyBZ9Mw
How to make an ebook cover in Microsoft Word (Part 2)
https://www.youtube.com/watch?v=dBX8Ue5tAqk
How to make a Kindle book cover in MS Word (3)
https://www.youtube.com/watch?v=7H2sN7rvbtA

11. If you will do a print edition, start the Print Cover Design process at the same time.

Just in case you're planning a print edition as well as an ebook, find out how much extra it will cost for the designer of your chosen cover to create a print book cover complete with back cover and spine.

If you decide to get a custom cover, determine the cost of a complete package with ebook and print cover.

Furnish the trim size you chose for the print book. You will need to send the designer more information later, but if you can get a bundle price initially, it will usually save you money.

12. Contract with an editor.

Never, ever rely on spell checks and grammar checks alone. For one thing, they often miss words that sound the same as the one you meant to use. The applications won't catch words that you left out, words that were meant to be deleted when you made a correction, or words that you used several times in a paragraph. Only the human eye can catch those problems. That's where the value of an editor becomes apparent.

Writers are often confused about what kinds of editing their manuscript needs, and in what order. Part of the confusion stems from the different names free-lance editors use to describe their editing services. This confusion is made worse due to disagreement among industry professionals about the number of editing stages. These range from three to five, with very blurry lines between them, but one professional organization has set their standard at four types (I give as many names for each step as I know about).

These are:

- Developmental / Project editing (sometimes called manuscript evaluation, overview, or critique)
- Substantive / Content / Structural / Language editing (some editors call this stage Line Editing)
- Copy / Line / Mechanical editing
- Proofreading

Developmental editing is a bird's eye or macro look at the themes, content, and structure of your book.

In the traditional publishing world, editors work with the author to produce a publishable book. Authors might need guidance in organizing their material, staying on track with their content, and meeting deadlines. Developmental editors identify problems with the plot in fiction books, and guide authors through the process of taking raw material and turning it into readable and compelling text in nonfiction titles.

A developmental editor helps you identify the story problem your main character must resolve. They may suggest that you change the point of view of the overall book from first person to third person, or vice versa. They may suggest you add or delete a subplot, or delete scenes that don't advance the plot. They may even tell you to write additional scenes to develop characters more fully, or to clarify plot points.

You're not usually going to run into the need for a developmental editor, because in the indie author's world, you can use critique partners and/or beta readers to help with this sort of editing, if necessary. You might need such help if you've been struggling with a manuscript that doesn't work. In such a case, you could send early drafts of the book, a partial draft, or a completed first draft to your editor or your beta readers for their input. I won't address sending partial copies to editors or readers in this book.

Substantive editing is usually done on a complete first draft of the book. It's what many writers picture as the job of an editor, where the red pen (or track changes) comes out and the manuscript drips blood from being gutted and rearranged. The editor (or beta readers) identifies problems in structure, coherence, consistency, plot flow, and character development. The point of this stage is to make the book readable and understandable.

This is the time to catch plot holes, discover if a secondary character should have more of a role, or keep focus more on the main action instead of side plots. It's more about details than developmental editing.

Copy editing usually occurs later in the indie publishing process where the framework of the book is set. It doesn't take a deep dive into the structure or content of the book. Instead, it's about details: spelling, punctuation, grammar, syntax and word usage. This keeps your author voice intact.

Copy editors, also called line editors, go through manuscripts to correct not just grammar and sentence structure but also to improve the flow of ideas and to resolve inconsistencies. Copy editors need an exceptional eye for catching errors and the patience to wade through manuscripts line by line.

Proofreading is not really editing, per se. It's the *last* step in the editing process before a final revision, not, as sometimes new writers believe, the *first* step. It takes place when a book has been formatted or typeset, so it's actually a part of the book production phase. Proofreaders look for typos, correct errors that escaped the editor or writer, check the layout, font, headers and footers, and generally make sure the book will present your best work.

It's not the time for you to include another great quote or scene at the proofreading stage. Do that before you send your manuscript out. Rest assured that the proofreader isn't going to make any substantive changes. Proofreading is merely the final hedge against embarrassment.

It's up to you to decide what kind of editing you will need when the time comes, and to find an editor who will fit your needs. Get recommendations from your author friends or search online.

Here are three editors I recommend:

Maria Hoagland (also formats both e- and print books). http://www.mariahoagland.com/editing.html

Tamara Hart Heiner offers several types of editing services. http://tamarahartheiner.blogspot.com/p/copy-editing-rates.html

Karen Hoover of Tin Bird Publications and Author Services is a content and line editor. She also does both ebook and print book formatting, and offers an extensive list of other author services. https://www.tinbirdpub.net/editing-services

Get references from authors who have used the editor before you sign a contract (ask the editor for references). Also, find out if your schedule timelines will work together. Sometimes, having a deadline because the editor's slot is set in stone is an incentive to get everything done in time. You probably know whether this would work for you, or if you need a more flexible schedule on the editor's part.

Let the editor you propose to contract with know what kind of editing you're looking for and determine what their charges will be. Ask for an editing sample to see if your styles mesh. Only once you have all questions answered should you sign a contract.

13. Finish the First Draft.

Now that you have the software you will need and have set up vital accounts, go back to work and finish the First Draft. Label it as your First Draft. Maybe Title_1stDraft will do it. You could also include the date, if you want: Title_1stDraft_2017-03-14. Save it in the project folder on your computer.

Chapter 2
SECOND DRAFT: Shining and Sharing

1. Check for misspellings and other boo-boos.

If you're following My Way, do the following for your Second Draft work.

Make a copy of your First Draft or Save-As, changing the title to something like *Title_2ndDraft*. This is the file you will use as you work on the Second Draft.

Okay, why should you save the file with another name? It's good practice to save each major change as its own file. This preserves the copy of your first draft, in case you decide you don't like your changes—or need some text you deleted and regret losing.

The work on the second draft consists of fixing stuff that I didn't address in my First Draft, and preparing to send the raw material out to my very trusted Beta Readers. I'm going to correct misspellings; check for and eliminate "pet words;" find, fix and eliminate writing notes and scene titles I may have left in the manuscript; and make my word usage consistent.

As I mentioned in Chapter 1, I use a free writers program called yWriter5 created by Simon Haynes. I write all my First Drafts using the program. I love that the basic unit is a scene. I can tackle that much with no problem.

You can get the full story on yWriter at

http://spacejock.com,

where you can also download the program, totally free. When I say free, I also mean without any virii or other malware. Simon is a good guy, and has made his programs free (yes, he's created many others), except for one, which brings in some well-deserved cash. You probably won't have need of that program as a writer. Feel free to take advantage of Simon Haynes's good heart and download yWriter5 or yWriter 6. Or not, if you have something else or are satisfied with your current word processing program.

Once my First Draft has been written, I export it to Word to continue. There are other ways of managing manuscripts through yWriter5, but remember, this is My Way of doing things. Up to this time, I've used the parts of yWriter that I feel comfortable with.

So, at this point, I'm in Word, and I run an initial spell-check. This will find the words that Word thinks I've misspelled. I don't and can't rely alone on Word, since I often write a bit of dialect that makes Word huffy and hypersensitive. But I do run the completed First Draft through the spell-check. That's good enough for now.

On to "pet words," which are those words I frequently use when I'm being a lazy writer. You know: *just, only, very, some,* and the like. I do a global search and get rid of those little scamps, rewriting with better attention to my language. I have my list of pet words to find, and you should develop your own, so you can search and destroy them at this stage. You'll find that the more aware you are of your pet words, the fewer times you'll have to weed them out in the Second Draft.

Sometimes as I'm writing, I will run across the need to do a little bit of research. I don't always stop writing to check out the facts (because, well, my tendency once I've stopped to do research is to keep researching until I forget I'm supposed to be writing). I usually wait until I've finished the day's writing to do the research. To help me find the place where I need help, I insert square brackets and a short note to myself, usually including the letters "TK," like this: [TK when did the Mexican War begin?] At the end of the day I go find out about the Mexican War, then put in what is needed. If I might have forgotten to delete all such notes, during my Second Draft work I make sure by searching for TK. Using TK is an old trick attributed to German printers. The upper-case letters TK don't usually occur together in the English language, nor, evidently, in the German language.

yWriter5 prompts the user to title each scene, the basic unit in most fiction and thus, in the software. These titles could range from the simple Scene 1 to the more descriptive one I put on this scene: SECOND DRAFT: Shining and Sharing. That will probably be my Chapter title, but if I have scene titles that are not going to be a permanent part of my manuscript, here's my chance to get rid of them, now that I'm using Word.

I have a list of compound words I use frequently in my writing. I pull it out at Second Draft time so I can check my word usage in the current project. Have I used "well spoken" in one part of my First Draft and "well-spoken" in another? How about "hand-crafted" versus "hand crafted"? I check out those inconsistencies now. You might want to start making your own list as you go through your First Draft.

When I have finished all the touch up work above, I'm finished with my Second Draft file, which I save, of course.

2. Make a copy of the Second Draft for Beta Readers.

By now, you should have your list of four or five people, the Beta Readers, that you trust to read through your manuscript and make suggestions and/or find mistakes, plot holes, and lack of character development. You need to prepare a manuscript file to send to them, along with instructions of what you expect them to do.

You should choose your beta readers for various strengths. One may be terrific at seeing the overall structure of your story. Another may be awesome at catching unnecessary scenes, or seeing where you left a needed scene out. You don't need someone whose major strength is proofreading at this point, because you haven't finished your work. You will be doing certain amounts of re-writing still, so proofreading would be wasted now.

Keep in mind that beta readers are doing you a huge favor, and treat them accordingly. I always send them an autographed print copy of the novel on which they gave me their valuable time and their opinions and suggestions.

Take your finished Second Draft and make a copy. Rename it Title_for Beta Readers, Title_4BR, or something like that. Save in the appropriate folder.

In your beta reader file, include a copyright notice, just as a gentle reminder that these are your words. Then either include instructions on what feedback you want from them right there in the manuscript, or do it on the cover email when you send it out.

Here's the copyright notice I put on the beta reader copy for one of my novels:

THE ZION TRAIL
A Novel

Copyright © 2015 Marsha Ward

Then I launched right into Chapter 1. I gave instructions in the email.

Here's another "Copyright Page," which includes brief instructions for the beta readers:

Gone for a Soldier
The Owen Family Saga

Marsha Ward

© 2014 Marsha Ward

Please make your comments, corrections, suggestions, etc., by using a method that suits you, such as Track Changes, putting your comments where they occur in another color type, or another method of your choosing (let me know how that works, please).

Before you email the file back with your comments, please change the filename by doing a "save-as" and adding some identifier, such as your initials or name.

You have until July 31st to complete your reading and evaluation of the work. If you finish before that time, feel free to send the file back early.

Save the file for your beta readers.

3. Send Manuscript to Beta Readers.

I generally give beta readers three to four weeks to accomplish the reading, make suggestions, change the file name, and return the file to me. Any longer than that, and they may put off the reading task, but if they are eager to read the work, a short deadline will give them an added incentive to get started. Always be mindful of their schedule.

Here's the email I sent out with one novel. In this instance, I asked my beta readers to find typos, among other tasks, and specified a return date. I also suggested ways they could make their suggestions, correct typos, etc.:

Hello!

Your assignment, should you choose to accept it, is to read this manuscript as though it were a book, and email it back to me with any comments by or before July 31. Please let me know if that is not doable with your schedule.

You might have special editing talents, and if so, find the typos, misspelled words, the repeated words, the identical words close together, the plot holes, words I misused, etc. Do make sure that I say dinner when I'm referring to the midday meal, and supper as the one at night, because I may have slipped up a time or two.

There are Spanish phrases interspersed here and there. If you are fluent in the language and find errors in syntax, accents, etc., let me know, because I suspect I've forgotten to proof read a couple of places that I essentially dashed off at the time. If you do not know Spanish, let me know if anything is not cleared up through surrounding comments.

You may use Track Changes, if you know how, or simply insert your comments in a different color or font. You can write at the bottom of the manuscript. Go ahead. Whatever method works for you.

You'll note that I used MS Word 2003 for this version, so let me know if you cannot open it and I'll try something else.

My overriding consideration is that you read this book as though you were a reader. Not a writer. Not an editor. An everyday reader. Please answer the following three statements:

1. I liked what I read.

2. I quit reading on page [　].

3. I liked what I read and I would have bought this.

If anything in the manuscript disturbs you greatly, please make a note of what that is (and any suggestions as to how you would change it), because I know this story is sometimes quite dark in tone, and includes depictions of physical abuse. If you don't think you can handle that, please let me know now.

Thank you so much for your offer to be a Reader. I do esteem you highly!

Sincerely,
Marsha Ward

In that email, I gave examples of what feedback I wanted, including three statements to answer. The things you want to know may be more extensive.

You could ask if the story held their interest from the start, and if not, why not. You might ask about if they related to the main character and prompt them to answer if they could feel the character's pain or excitement. You might ask about their interest in the setting, and if descriptions were vivid and real. Did the story began to lag or lose their interest? Exactly where did that occur? Were there confusing parts? Annoying or frustrating parts? Which parts and why?

Were there discrepancies or inconsistencies in places, character details, timelines, other details that didn't connect to the whole story? Were the characters believable? Were there too many of them to keep track, or characters with similar names?

Was there enough conflict and tension to keep their interest? Was the ending believable and satisfying? (Endings don't have to be *happy*, but they should give a reader a sense of satisfactory completion.)

One class of details that matters most to me to know is if certain scenes didn't work or seemed unnecessary, and perhaps more telling, did I leave out (or avoid writing) scenes that I should have included?

You always want to let your beta reader know what you expect. Let them know it's best to give honest feedback, even if they're afraid you will see it as negative. Stress to them that negative opinions won't hurt your feelings. This avoids a situation where you get back broad and unhelpful comments like, "I loved the book!" "Keep up the good work," or "Not your best novel." They are entitled to their opinions of the manuscript, positive or negative, and concrete feedback will help you make any corrections or re-writes you agree with.

Now, prepare an email (or do separate emails for each beta reader), include your instructions and deadline, attach the manuscript file, and send it off. Be sure to note in your spreadsheet to whom and when your emails went out. Check back with them within a day or two to make sure they received your beta reader file, if the file opened, and if your instructions are clear.

4. Set release dates for ebook and print edition.

While you are waiting to hear back from your beta readers, you have work to do. Set a release date for the ebook. Make it about three months from now. Set a date for the print edition for about a month later.

There's much debate among writers about what the optimal time of the month or day of the week is best for releasing books. Some say early is good and that releases should take place on a Tuesday. Some prefer to release books on Fridays.

In 2016, I released all my projects on a Friday. Why? Because I have had a feature on my blog for several years called "Fresh Book Friday," and I wanted to feature *my* new books on their release day. Simple as that. I've also released books on Tuesdays or on my wedding anniversary, or just when the book was ready to go. I also haven't made a big fuss about releases or launches lately. Not after I spent beaucoup bucks on prizes for a big Release Party, plenty of money for a blog tour, and other efforts to make a big splash, and didn't see a difference in sales between making a Big Hoorah and doing quiet, or "soft" releases.

In the end, I don't think it matters if you make a huge event out of a release or not, as long as your books are solidly written and sufficient mention is made of the release dates to the most important people in your author life: your readers and other loyal fans. Yes, go ahead and crank up the publicity and word-of-mouth machines, but my advice, if you want to publish your book My Way, is that you not spend a lot of time, effort, or money on actual or virtual release parties. But that is totally up to you.

5. Decide on prices for ebook and print editions.

I price my novel ebooks around $3.99 to $4.99, depending on length. I'll do a couple of sales during the year, reducing the price anywhere from half-off to ninety-nine cents, for a limited time. Usually I do such sales on the first book of a series. During "Read an eBook Week," however, which occurs during the first full week of March, I may discount all my novels. I sometimes do the same during the entire month of July, for a "Summer/Winter" sale that Smashwords.com sponsors, celebrating the onset of the pertinent season in both hemispheres of the world.

As to print books, I like to price them at a reasonable cost for readers. No twenty-five dollar books from this author! My price is $13.99 for novels from 50,000 to 80,000 words, and $14.99 for novels from 81,000 to 105,000 words. I haven't written any novels longer than that, so far.

Now is a good time to think about where you will be selling your print books, and if you will adjust prices when you hand sell them. Many writers set up launch parties for new releases, or attend established events, like book fairs and conferences.

I go to a limited number of events during a year's time. Unless a bookstore is handling sales at the event, I price the books in whole dollars at five-dollar marks, in order not to have to deal with coins or one-dollar bills in making change. For example, if a book costs $16.95, I'll charge $15. If a book costs $12.95, I'll charge $10.00. This nets me enough per book to pay for my author copy and a little extra, plus gets new readers started on what I hope is a craving for my work. I also may give a discount on a set of novels, like $50 for five novels, which saves a reader a good chunk of change.

Increasingly, folks don't carry cash at events, so I also take a credit card reader that syncs with an app on my cell phone.

Around town, I have friends who buy print copies of my books when they come out. I keep a special bag at hand that contains cash: five- and one-dollar bills to give them change, usually for a twenty-dollar bill. As I said, I deal in whole dollar figures when I hand sell. I round up to the next dollar figure, or if I'm in a good mood, down to the lower dollar amount. I don't get complaints on either charge.

If I'm planning to re-print a physical book with changes, like a new cover or added bonus material, I'll discount the existing edition drastically to reduce inventory.

6. Make decisions on business set-up.

Indie Publishing is a business. Yes, I hear you groaning. That's a fact of life, and if you have income from your book (which you and I are both pulling for), you'll need to prepare yourself to deal with taxes on that income. I'm not going to address the ins and outs of the Internal Revenue Service in this book, but I will advise you to take care of legal necessities.

Check with your state to see if you need to register a business name or if it requires you to have a DBA or Doing-Business-As filing. Unless you're selling books out of your home or off a business/publisher website, you probably don't need a business license and/or a tax license, but it pays to check it out and be sure. *Don't cheat!*

Decide if you want to have a publishing or imprint name in your books. To me, it looks more professional to have "Published by WestWard Books" on my title page than having nothing. Am I a publisher snob? Who knows. It just looks better to me, because some people still judge indie authors as inferior. That's not true, but I started when the only game in town was traditional publishing, so maybe having a publication house of my own to publish my books is ingrained in me. Maybe if I had fifty more years of writing life in me, I wouldn't bother.

Your state may require you to incorporate to operate as a business, so check that out. Otherwise, you can set up as a "Sole Proprietor." Get educated where you need to know this stuff.

The most important thing is to *treat* your writing as a business, and *not to neglect* the legal realities.

To keep your everyday money separate from your book income, set up a checking account, credit card, and PayPal account in your author or business name. This gives you an instant view of your income and tracks your expenses, and will really help come tax time.

Another thing to consider is if you will buy International Standard Book Numbers, or ISBNs, for short. I do, because I use a publishing name. You don't have to, and can use the free ISBNs available from Smashwords and CreateSpace when necessary, if you keep in mind the rules of the usage from these distributors. Some online vendors don't require them. Amazon has their own numbers, called ASINs. You don't need an ISBN on your book to qualify it for bestseller lists, if that's your desire. There's a trend in thinking in the indie publishing world that ISBNs are outmoded. I'm beginning to buy into that theory, but you do as you wish. Just don't go to the Bowker website (the only place in the U.S. where you can purchase ISBNs that are yours) at

http://myidentifiers.com

and get swept into their need for you to buy all sorts of extras. You don't need their barcode. CreateSpace will put one on your book for free.

If you do purchase your own ISBNs, Bowker will send you an email, which includes a list of your ISBNs. Print this out and keep it in a safe place. You will need it later in this process.

A third item for your consideration is whether or not you will register your copyright.

I choose to do so on my major works, because I have a friend who has been embroiled in a lawsuit against a plagiarizer for a couple of years now. One thing I've learned through her process is that the amount of damages one can seek is much higher with a properly and timely registered copyright. See more information on online copyright registration in the United States at

https://www.copyright.gov/registration/.

7. Start mentioning your book.

If you haven't mentioned your book to anyone yet, now is the time to start tooting your horn. I know. It's difficult. Writers, along with other creatives (that's the new buzzword: creatives), are traditionally shy.

But during the six weeks before the anticipated release date, it's time to ramp up mentions of your upcoming book via social media, your blog or website, your newsletter, and other contacts. If you have your own publisher website, use it for coming book mentions.

This is the time to ask your family, friends, and contacts to share your book mentions by, well, Sharing and Re-Tweeting and however else they can spread the word.

Just a bit of advice about social media. You *do not* have to have an account on every kind of social media that's out there. Pick one or two, and use them well. Be consistent. Make friends and contacts. *Do. Not. Spam!*

I favor Facebook, myself. It has become important in several areas of my life, not only as a writer's tool. I occasionally tweet via Twitter. I have a LinkedIn Account, but it's been ages since I peeked at it. I think I show up on GoodReads about quarterly. LibraryThing? Eek! It's been *years!*

I really have enough to do trying to keep my life, my writing, my website, and my newsletter going.

I suspect you may have the same challenges.

My mother always advised us to KISS: Keep it Simple, Silly. Yes, she thought "silly" was nicer than the alternate. I'm giving you the same advice. You have plenty to do already to follow My Way through Indie Publishing. Remember, concerning social media, KISS.

8. Get Beta Reader comments back.

The renamed manuscripts with comments from beta readers should start to trickle in. You should keep some kind of table or spreadsheet on what they say. If your beta readers used Track Changes and you're brave, you can merge all their documents into one, full of comments. (No, I don't have experience in doing this. One of my writer friends comes to my rescue every time I need help with Track Changes. Make sure you have such mentors.)

Back to what the beta readers tell you. For example, these are some of the comments I received on one novel.

"Why does the family own two horses? You might give a reason," then the reader elaborated with suggestions.

"I love the language. It gives a real feel for the historical time and setting of the story."

"Give some rumors of cholera being about before..." something happened. "Build up to it." (Three of my beta readers mentioned the need for a build up to this situation. That was enough for me. I complied with their wishes.)

"I love love love love love the book." That high praise came with caveats. This reader wanted me to flesh out emotions in spots where she felt I had rushed. She wanted more expansion of a character and more evidence of a romance. She wanted the family to feel a loss and show more upset reactions. In another place, she wanted an event to rip out her heart. Through her comments, she pushed me to work harder on the novel, to write a bigger, better book.

This is the type of reaction and feedback you want from your beta readers. Soon you will act on their feedback, using what seems right for the project.

Chapter 3
THIRD DRAFT

1. Incorporate changes from Beta Readers

Touch up your manuscript, incorporating suggested changes from Beta Readers—that you agree with—into the manuscript.

Feedback from Beta Readers is valuable, to the extent that you agree with their assessment of your work. If you asked your readers for significant input, this step may take you several days. It all depends on what you get back and if you agree with changes they suggest. If the job is simply correcting typos, reworking words that are repeated in close proximity to each other, and deleting repeated words (like two uses of "and" in a row), it's a piece of cake.

Be sure you have thanked your beta readers for their assistance. You don't have to tell them whether anything they suggested is useful or not. A simple "Thank you for your help" is sufficient.

2. Decide if you will use book sales tracking sites.

You might consider at this time whether it is important to you to use a service that tracks book sales for you. Such sites usually charge a fee to report to you daily on your sales. There are several of them, some of which only report on Kindle sales, and some of which track your book's rank and ratings. It's necessary to keep track of the money coming in, but often we obsess about rankings and ratings, and this obsession can tear the heart out of our writing time. Since income is the only number that really matters, I don't recommend seeking out services whose stock-in-trade is giving book rankings and ratings on Amazon.

Ask yourself if you have enough books (and enough sales of them) to warrant the cost of having a daily email sent to you, or if you are content to check sales on your own. Occasionally. (You do this through the dashboard of the online retailer to which you have uploaded your book.) If this is your first book, I advise against using a sales tracker service. As you get more product to track, such a service may become useful. If you do sales promotions in the future, tracking sales may be useful in order to see if and by what degree the promotion has increased your book sales. You can still do this by yourself.

BookTrakr, found at

http://booktrakr.com,

informs you of sales on all your upload sites. Here's a link to an overview of a few different tracking services' sites, including a review of BookTrakr, which the author found to be his favorite:

https://kindlepreneur.com/book-sales-tracker/

TrackerBox, from StoryBox Software

http://www.storyboxsoftware.com/tdownload.htm,

is tracking software. It has a 45-day free trial, and costs ninety dollars. It does keep track of a long list of sales sites, if you uploaded to them, but I know nothing about the product. Check it out, if you think this is a need, not a want.

Book Report, found here

https://www.getbookreport.com/,

is a bookmarklet that reports on Kindle sales. It has a unique pricing structure: free for a two-week trial, free for everyone earning less than $1000 a month on KDP, and $10 a month or $100 a year if you've completed your free trial and earned more than $1000.00 the last month. This is a simple system. Once the bookmarklet is put onto your browser's bookmarks bar and you're logged into the Reports page of your KDP dashboard, click the Book Report icon in your bookmarks bar, and watch what happens. I haven't learned how to work the comparison section yet, but that's less of a necessity to me (and besides, comparing yourself to other authors is just insanity), and I've been busy writing this book to help y'all out, and...

If you want more information about book tracking services and software, Google "book sales trackers," visit the websites, and gather information.

Chapter 4
FOURTH DRAFT: Appearance

1. Clean up your punctuation and spacing.

I'm a perfectionist, so I'm going to use this space to go on a bit about punctuation consistency. That matters to me in the appearance department. It's up to you to decide whether it matters so much to you or not.

I like to have all my punctuation sitting up and barking at my command. Okay, what I mean is, I like all the quotation marks to be consistent, not some "curly" and some "straight," as may happen when you begin writing in one software and then edit in another. You'll have to decide which way you want yours. Curly looks good in a print book, but straight is perfectly acceptable in an ebook. However, I've seen it both ways in ebooks (and sometimes, both ways in the same book!). Make the choice, and go through with a global search and replace, changing the quotation marks that aren't consistent with that choice.

I also find that some bad typing habits can cause unanticipated problems that can be solved. I'm looking at you, spaces!

Remember back in high school typing class? (Okay, maybe you didn't take typing.) Or if you are self-taught? Or if you learned about manuscript formatting back in the olden days? Many ancient typists (I'm talking about me) were taught that the proper spacing after a sentence was two taps with the thumb.

Not any more, ladies and gentlemen. As computers came into wide usage, we had more fonts available than mono-space Courier. Proportional fonts made two spaces between sentences unnecessary. Two taps with the thumb went out the window.

Here's a compound word from me about using the space bar to create indentations and for centering text. UH-UH! Another couple of words from yours truly about letting that thumb keep hitting the space bar when a paragraph comes along. NO WAY!

Spaces do not make consistent indentations. They do not serve you well for centering text. Learn about the Paragraph function in Word, which controls text placement, such as indentations and centering text.

Be aware of the nuisance factor of extra spaces after the period at the end of a paragraph. You usually don't even see them when you're working on your manuscript, unless you have the "Show/Hide" control turned on. However, they can cause a big gap between paragraphs in your book when the finished product is read on an ereader. Your reader will blame any and all formatting problems they encounter on you. If you have too many problems with your format, somebody is going to complain in a review. Such negative reviews about formatting can cause losses in sales.

Appearance matters! This draft is your chance to clean up any punctuation inconsistencies.

2. Have a professional author photo taken.

While we're talking about Appearance, I must mention that your face is going to appear all over the Internet and the Book World, so now is the time to get a professional photographer to take your picture for your Author Photo. This is a big step. It will require the outlay of some money, but do take the step. It's well worth it.

Ask other local writers who they recommend. Check writers' conferences that you are likely to attend. Some arrange for a photographer to be on scene to take photos for you at a reasonable cost. I know the American Night Writers Association (ANWA) writers conference in Arizona has done this. It's likely that other conferences make this service available.

3. Get informed about Authorgraph.

Authorgraph is a free service that allows readers to acquire an author's autograph for their ebooks. Found at

http://www.authorgraph.com/,

Authorgraph used to be called Kindlegraph, and still requires that the author have one or more books listed on KDP so the service can find them. But authorgraphs can be read on whatever device the reader owns. The Authorgraph service fills the emotional need of both the reader to have and the author to provide a signed, personalized greeting related to an ebook. Nifty, huh?

Here's how it works: A reader browses and finds a book for which they want an authorgraph, or is alerted through a widget on the author's website. They request the authorgraph, and when the author fulfills the request, they get an email to view it. While authorgraphs are related to the author's book, they are separate documents.

Visit the site and gather information, then decide if you will use Authorgraph. If you want to use it, once your ebook is published and showing on Amazon, set up your account. At that time, you can download the personalized widget from Authorgraph to put on your website. The widget lists your book or books, letting your readers know that you offer this service.

If you already have a book or books available, you can open an account now and list your ebooks.

Chapter 5
SEND TO EDITOR

1. Send your polished manuscript to your editor.

At this point, your manuscript should be polished enough to send off to the editor of your choice. Make sure you discuss the services you require, and agree upon a deadline for the return of the manuscript. See Chapter 1, Section 12 to refresh your memory of the services editors can provide.

2. Get the edited manuscript back.

The editor is a member of your publishing team. The edits your editor makes will likely give you substantial help in the areas for which you asked for assistance. Now you will incorporate into your manuscript the changes the editor suggested, if you agree with those changes.

Remember, this is your book. If you have a serious disagreement with any of the edits, or can't bear to make suggested changes, that's up to you. It's also *on* you, in terms of the polished whole of your book, so think twice about whether you know more about grammar or spelling or structure than the editor does before you reject suggestions out of hand.

Take time to consider each suggestion in light of your knowledge and skill levels. That word you want to keep may not actually mean what you think it means!

It doesn't matter how you do this part of the process, whether you combine the files with Track Changes and hope you know how to accept or reject the changes from your editor, or copy and replace the parts you like from your editor's version into your master file. At any rate, change the file name to include 4th-Draft and save it frequently as you work.

Chapter 6
FIFTH DRAFT: Final Book Block

1. Print out the manuscript to read aloud.

When the Fifth Draft is finished, it will be your Final Book Block, and you want it to be as perfect as you can make it. Open the 4th Draft file and rename it to include the word FINAL.

Bear in mind that every book that is published has some error or another in it somewhere. There may be more than one in your manuscript. The beauty of independently publishing your work is that when you find a mistake, or a reader points one out, you can pretty easily make a correction and upload the corrected file. However, you want to do your due diligence to find and eliminate every mistake you can before uploading for that first publication.

To this end, print out your manuscript now and read it through to find the errors and the places to which you might want to give a last-minute edit. Enter any changes you want to make. Mark them in some colorful way, like highlighting on the print-out, so you can find all your corrections later.

When you're finished, read the book again. Aloud.

You can opt to have your computer read it to you while you follow along, or have someone else read to you, if you have an obliging spouse or friend.

The purpose of this exercise is to get your ears as well as your eyes involved with your perfection-seeking. You'll be surprised at how your relationship to your manuscript changes. Hearing it helps to bring it alive—and helps you find a few errors no one else found.

How do I get my computer to read to me?

I use a PC with Windows 7 and Word 2010. If you have a similar product, you need to activate the Text to Speech function already in Word. Here's a great YouTube video that explains how to do that:

https://www.youtube.com/watch?v=ips3k6UdY7Q

I activated this function some time ago, and have found it *so* useful in editing. It's too bad Microsoft doesn't have it on the Word toolbar as a standard feature!

Make the changes you need on your printed manuscript. Remember, mark each change loudly, well, visually, so you'll find each of them later. Then make a log of where the errors occur.

2. Make corrections to your manuscript file and rename it.

Now open your FINAL file and transfer the changes from the print-out to this file. Save.

Take a deep breath. You're doing an awesome job. You have this!

3. Add Front Matter to the file.

Now you're ready to add other information to your book.

Ebook design is constantly changing, as indie authors try out and share new concepts that seem to work. One of the increasingly standard elements is a brief book description at the very beginning.

Why on earth?

This has come about because so many voracious readers download many, many ebooks, some free, some for ninety-nine cents, for whatever reason readers buy a book.

However, the great majority of the time, these books don't get read right away, so some smart person started putting the book's description at the beginning, as a reminder of what the book was all about. Readers liked it. Other authors followed suit.

I do the same thing in my books now. Here's an example:

Wes Haught wants his brother to grow up and take on his share of the chores at the family's general store. Lonnie Haught dreams of the day he can leave home and use his gun. Both brothers resent the added work their father's recent accident has laid on them.

When a new family arrives in Haught Springs, Wes falls for the fair-haired daughter, while Lonnie seizes upon the father's offer of a job as his chance for escape.

But lies unravel and lives hang in the balance as brother fights against brother.

Fiery emotions and vengeful acts erupt in a smoldering Western adventure novella from the author of the acclaimed Owen Family Saga.

Next come the title page elements:

Blood at Haught Springs

Men of Haught Springs #1

Marsha Ward

Published by WestWard Books at Smashwords

That is followed by my copyright page information:

Copyright 2016 Marsha Ward

Cover Design by Linda Boulanger
http://www.telltalebookcovers.weebly.com

In truth, the book description, the title page, and the copyright page blend together pretty much in a continuous flow.

Go explore a few ebooks you've downloaded, and pull some printed books off your bookshelves, too. You're looking for information, format, and style. What do the authors/publishers include on the title page? Well, the title and author, of course, but in what form do they appear? Is the title in all capital letters or mixed capitals and lower-case letters? This may depend a bit on the genre of each book, but get a general idea of how other people do this so you can decide what you want appearing in your book.

You may want to increase the size of the font for the title a few points, that is, from 12-point Times New Roman to 14- or 16-point TNR. Don't go overboard. Most vendors give you cautions on this subject, as there are technical limitations on the size of font you can use for ebooks. And remember, the reader can change your font size to suit themselves. They can also change the font, so it's best to stick to a basic font like Times New Roman for fiction or Arial, for nonfiction.

You probably want to center the title and author name, but you can address that later when you're formatting, or ask that your formatter center the title page text for you.

Some title pages include the words "A Novel." I've heard people complain lately about those words showing up on covers, but no discussion of them being on a title page. It's up to you whether you want to include them or not. Basically, a title page should give the title, the series, if any, and the author's name. You can add the publisher name you've chosen to use, if you have made that choice, at the bottom of the title page.

Once you have put in the book description and the basic information on the title page, the next thing you need to insert is the copyright page. Some indie authors include the publisher name somewhere on this page, too.

Back in Chapter 2, Section 2, you saw the two examples I gave of copyright notices:

Copyright/symbol/year/person, and

symbol/year/person.

My personal choice has changed as I've standardized my configuration. I've phased out using the copyright symbol in ebooks. Sometimes it doesn't play well with the formatting of some vendors, and it's not a legal necessity. Therefore, I recommend that your copyright page begin with simply "Copyright 2017 Your Name" because that's simple and clear. You saw that in my example above. Under that, I sometimes put a hyperlink or at least the text of the link to my website, marshaward.com. Whether or not I use a hyperlink depends on how many distractions I want to introduce into the book right away. Nowadays, I tend to put the website link in the Back Matter at the end of the book.

Underneath my copyright notice, I put whatever notice my cover designer requires. This may be as simple as an acknowledgement of their work, or as complex as designated text and hyperlink.

"Cover Design by" so-and-so is a simple and elegant notice.

Next, you may want to put in a notice of reservations of your rights, as I did in the example of copyright page information above. It is standard to warn readers that you hold all rights and ask that they respect them. Give some leeway for reviews, though. You want reviews!

I'll talk about creating a standard configuration for your ebooks in Chapter 9, Section 1.

When you have finished adding the extra pages, be sure to save your file.

Chapter 7
FOLDERS, FILES, AND ENDORSERS

1. Figure out folder structure.

Depending on how you decide to distribute your book, you will make various versions of your manuscript file. Be sure to label each file clearly for its particular purpose, and then put each one in a clearly labeled folder in your computer. These folders could include Ebook, Print Book, Copyright, Endorsers, eARCs, one each for your ebook vendors, etc. I'll mention these again in each section.

2. Final Book Block File Copies

Make two copies of the Final Book Block file. Rename one to include "ebook" and one "print book," such as "MobyDick_final-ebook" and "MobyDick_final-print".

Put the files into folders called EBook and Print Book.

3. Edit EBook File to avoid weird formatting.

I take a step in my final ebook editing that you may find to be optional. I edit the ebook file to change Word's ellipses character and em-dashes to a special ebook format, which prevents problems from cropping up in ebook readers. Then I save the file to the EBook folder.

Here's why I take this extra step: Reading a book on an ereader gives the reader lots of advantages. They can pick the font, the size, and even the color. But when they make changes like these, the text of the book will adjust, or flow. Yes, it's a huge advantage for the reader, but if you created a book with lots of ellipses or em-dashes, you might get complaints in reviews about poor formatting in your book.

You see, ellipses, that string of three dots/periods and spaces that either indicate missing text in a quote or a thought petering out at the end of a sentence (usually in dialogue), have a nasty habit of running over from one line to the next. You know, one or two of the dots on one line and the rest on the next. This is incredibly unsightly. Word tried to fix this problem in ordinary documents like letters or legal documents by creating a faux ellipsis that is a single character, that is, three dots smashed together. If you delete it, all three dots disappear. The problem is that you don't want a lot of stray code from Word hanging out in the bowels of your ebook.

Em-dashes, those long lines placed between phrases to indicate that the writer wants to include another bit of information, are right up next to the words on either side, which makes them act oddly when someone changes a font size in the ebook. A line could be unexpectedly short when em-dashes are in the mix, due to the em-dash-containing-phrase being forced onto the next line.

There is a fix to these two problems, taught to me by a writer friend. It's totally optional, though. You are not obliged to go through and change your ellipses and em-dashes just because I do.

However, if you're interested, here's what I do. Where I have inserted an ellipsis in my manuscript (those three dots, usually with spaces between), I substitute three dots just after the word, then a space, then the next word. This is how it looks:

Daisy sniffled as she whispered, "I don't want... to lose... his love."

There is little chance that a dot will stray from one line to the next with this setup. I suppose it *could* happen, but it's less likely to occur.

For em-dashes, I do similarly. I attach the em-dash to the last word, and leave a space afterward before I type the next word:

The lines on the ground— some parallel, some at odd angles— appeared to have been fashioned by some sort of scraper, possibly dragged behind a tractor.

These separated em-dashes won't cause short lines to appear in the text on an ereader.

You may choose to use my fix or not. It's up to you.

4. Create Folders as Needed.

Within the EBook folder, make folders labeled Copyright File, Endorsers, and eARCS. Make others for the online vendors or distributors you will use, e.g.: Smashwords, Kindle, Nook, iBooks, Kobo, D2D, etc.

5. Make Copyright Registration File (optional).

Using the ebook Final Book Block file, make a pdf for Library of Congress copyright registration, and put it into the Copyright File Folder. Rename the pdf to include only your book's title.

The Library of Congress needs a file containing the Final Book Block with a title and copyright page, but they don't need any sales information, book lists, or extra incentives you plan to put in as front or back matter. You will use this pdf file for Copyright Registration after the ebook is released.

Even if you don't plan to register your copyright, you will need a file similar to this one later, so go ahead and make it.

6. Prepare Other Formats for Endorsers.

You may be lucky enough to secure author friends who will read your book and write a short endorsement or blurb for you to use in your promotional materials and possibly on the back cover of your print edition. If so, use the Calibre software I had you download to prepare ePub and mobi formats from the file in the EBook folder. Put these files in the Endorsers Folder.

Make a copy of the pdf in the Copyright File Folder and save it to the Endorsers Folder. If you did not make a pdf file for copyright registration, make a pdf file now from the same file as above.

These files may not include your cover. If you didn't include it in your Calibre conversion file, you might wish to send a copy of your cover file to your endorsers, just so they get a look at what they're praising. If you haven't received or created your cover yet, don't worry about it.

7. Send File to Endorsers.

Email your manuscript to your Endorsers in their preferred ebook file format (see your spreadsheet, where you noted those preferences). Give them a time limit, perhaps a month, for reading and sending back an endorsement. Note dates of sending and returns. Put the endorsements in a safe place!

Chapter 8
EBOOK COVER

1. Check and Complete Requirements for EBook Cover.

By this time, you probably have your ebook cover design completed or have received it from your cover designer. This should be in the form of a jpg file, ideally two, in both high (300 pixels-per-inch or ppi) and medium (72 ppi) resolutions.

If the cover designer forgets to mention how their work should be attributed, ask for their preferred copyright information to include on the copyright page. Make sure this element is inserted into your book file.

Yes, I know this chapter is short. Very short. In fact, it's almost possible to skip over it if two pages stick together or you blink while reading the ebook version. However short it may appear, it's important that you know that by this time, you need those ebook cover files!

If your designer has only sent you a high-resolution jpg file, you may need to ask a buddy to help you make smaller, web-promo-suitable images from *a copy of the original,* because you don't want to send your 5-megabyte, 1800-pixel wide cover image to someone to use in the blog feature they are doing for you about your new book. They only need something about 400 pixels wide, at a maximum. Your cover image at 250 pixels wide is even better.

The resolution for images to be used on the Internet should be 72 ppi, like for covers uploaded to some ebook vendors, as opposed to the 300 minimum ppi you need for your print book, before the cover is made into a pdf file.

This goes for your author image, too. Get someone to shrink down *a copy of the original* to various widths, including some with your face cropped to a square (think Facebook Profile image). Never, ever tinker with the original of your author image or cover. *Always* make a copy of those images to play with, even if you know exactly what you're doing. *Especially* if you know exactly what you're doing!

Chapter 9
PREPARE FOR EBOOK FORMATTING

1. Create Standard EBook Configuration

Bearing in mind that ebooks contain three parts, Front Matter, Book Block, and Back Matter, create a standard configuration for the books you will write.

Front Matter may include the brief book description I talked about in Chapter 6, Section 3 and other preliminary elements: title page, copyright information, copyright information for cover designer, statement of rights and warnings, licensing statement, dedication, table of contents, and the like. The Book Block follows.

The book concludes with the Back Matter, which may include a bonus sneak peek of your next book, a thank you, an appeal for a review, a list of other books or link to your website book list, a link to subscribe to your mailing list, and information about you as the author, plus your social media links. These days, many writers prefer to put acknowledgments and author notes in the Back Matter, as well. They do this to allow more of the actual content of the book to show in the "Look inside" feature at Amazon, or in the sample percentage you can authorize a prospective reader to view at Smashwords.

It's helpful to take a look at ebooks from other authors in your genre. Check what kinds of things they put in their Front Matter, and what they include in the Back Matter. Look at recent books. Pay attention to your "reader mind" as it determines what you like and dislike about the various arrangements.

Write a "Configuration Master" document, a sort of template setting out what you want to include in your current and future books, and how you want the front and back matter information to appear: Centered? Left justified? All caps for your titles and author name, or mixed capitals and lower-case letters? These are things you must decide.

2. Copy the EBook Final Book Block file.

Rename it Final EBook File and save.

3. Add Front and Back Matter.

Put the front and back matter that you decided to use in your standard configuration document into the ebook file. Save.

4. Create and Apply Styles.

Create Styles for headings and various portions of your book and apply. See the Smashwords Style Guide if you are unfamiliar with styles.

Or take a look at this article on formatting that includes a great section on styles:

http://www.veronicasicoe.com/blog/2015/04/how-to-format-your-novel-for-smashwords/

I know it refers to Smashwords, but this is basic information for learning about formatting.

Rename and save your file. This is the Final Ebook File.

Chapter 10
EBOOK FORMATTING

1. Discover Specifications for Vendors.

Determine what specifications are required by each online vendor to which you plan to upload your book (Kindle, Nook, iBooks, Kobo, Smashwords, D2D, etc.). I use Smashwords as my ebook distributor to other vendors, so I only format two files: one for Kindle and one for Smashwords.

2. Read the Smashwords Style Guide.

If you find any instructions in the Smashwords Style Guide that are so daunting that you cannot understand and follow them, formatting your manuscript may not be the best choice for you. Read on for an alternative choice.

3. Contract with a Formatter.

If you doubt you can follow the Smashwords Style Guide, contract with a formatter to provide the files you need.

Smashwords provides a great list of both ebook formatters and cover designers. This was created by Smashwords' founder, Mark Coker, which is why it's called Mark's List. Here's the link:

https://www.smashwords.com/list

Several more people I know format ebooks. Here are three formatters I know personally.

Maria Hoagland also does print book formatting (which we'll discuss later), and editing, and offers combination prices and extras for reasonable fees. http://mariahoagland.com/formatting.html.

Lindzee Armstrong formats both ebooks and print books, and offers combo pricing. She also creates promotional materials, if you have an interest or need. http://www.lindzeearmstrong.com/author-services/formatting-services/

Karen Hoover of Tin Bird Publications and Author Services is an ebook formatter with a quick turn-around time. She lays out print books and offers content and line editing among her extensive list of author services. https://www.tinbirdpub.net/editing-services

Check what services formatters offer and their prices. Contact a few of them to see if your schedule and theirs fits (it usually doesn't take an experienced formatter very long to format a regular novel). Ask lots of questions.

Send your chosen formatter the Final Ebook File referenced in the previous chapter.

4. Make Copies and Format.

If you have confidence in your abilities, prepare to format individual file copies of your ebook for the various vendors (Kindle, Nook, iBooks, Kobo, Smashwords, D2D, etc.). Some use Word files. Some require other formats. Most ask you not to embed a cover image inside the Final eBook File.

You may choose to use the Smashwords Style Guide to format your ebook. If you use a lot of italics like I do, you may find this article of use. I know I did!

http://www.veronicasicoe.com/blog/2015/03/how-to-clean-up-your-manuscript-formatting-in-ms-word/

Veronica's article about Styles that I recommended back in Chapter 9, Section 4, links to the above one, so you might have read it already.

Make as many copies of the Final Ebook File as you need for direct uploads, and format each one.

Save each one to the appropriate vendor folder.

Chapter 11
ADVANCE READER COPIES (ARCs):
Reviewers and Bloggers

1. Make eARC Copy.

Advance Reader Copies, or, as they are commonly known in publishing circles, ARCs, are unedited copies of your book intended for those who will read your book "in advance of publication." These include reviewers, and nowadays, bloggers.

In traditional publishing, when the book manuscript has been set in print book configuration, it may not have been fully edited yet. Thus, it may or may not be exactly the same book as release-day readers will purchase.

In your case, you have a book that's very close to the final form, if not an exact copy. What you're going to send out to the reviewers and bloggers you enlisted at the beginning is an eARC, since this is the ebook version. It won't have the fancy characteristics of a print book. That's perfectly acceptable.

Make a copy of the Final eBook File (I use the Smashwords copy) and label it eARC. Save it to the eARC folder. Embed a medium resolution jpg file of the cover at the beginning of the file. Indicate above the Title Page that this is an "Uncorrected Advance Reader Copy."

A word about ARCs: If I *ever* hear you refer to them as *Advanced* Reader Copies, I will disavow ever knowing you. We must not discriminate against less advanced readers. Yes, my tongue is hovering somewhere around my cheek, but hearing an ARC called an *Advanced Reader Copy* is a huge cringe maker for me. Don't be the person who makes me cringe!

2. Create eARCs for Reviewers and Bloggers.

From the eARC Word file, create eARCs for reviewers and bloggers in the formats preferred by them: ePub, mobi, and pdf.

BE AWARE THAT SOME AUTHORS DO NOT PROVIDE PDF COPIES to unknown readers, as that format is easily sold to pirate sites. Know and trust the people to whom you send your eARCs. If you have signed up bloggers who are unknown to you, don't send them pdf files.

3. Send eARCs.

Send the eARCs—along with your jpg cover design file, if you did not embed a copy of the cover—to committed reviewers and bloggers. Inform them of the ebook release date and any special plans you have, such as the dates of cover reveals or blog tours.

Make sure you make a note in your team spreadsheet of when you send each person the eARC, and if/when you receive word back from them of a posted review, a blog post, and the like. It's always good to have complete records and files, if possible.

Chapter 12
PREPARE FOR UPLOADING

1. Receive all endorsements.

By this time, you probably are starting to receive the endorsements you requested from authors or other experts. If you did not ask anyone for endorsements, that's okay. Perhaps things your beta readers said can help you with the further steps in this process.

If you did ask for endorsements, make note of when you receive them back, and be sure to send these kind folks a warm thanks. If you plan to thank them with a print copy of your book or something similar, keep good notes so you won't skip that step. Make sure you have their mailing address!

Of equal importance, keep a record of what your endorsers say. You will use these comments in various ways. You might find a short "pull" quote or tidbit that's great to incorporate into the final front cover design of either or both ebook and print book, or more extensive quotes for back cover copy on your print book. One or more of these endorsements could be used in your book descriptions at online retailer sites.

Be aware that you can use parts of the quotes from the endorsers. You pick and choose what best suits your usage of the comments. You're not obligated to use long or complete quotations. Sometimes, the best use of an endorsement is a small part. Most helpful authors expect this and give you far more material than you need. I even received two separate endorsements for the same book from one really congenial author.

2. Create book description(s).

You will need enticing descriptions of what is in store for the reader for book detail pages at the online vendors. Read each vendor's rules and restrictions. If you use Smashwords as a distributor, for example, they require both a short and a long description.

Many authors think you should include a summary of the plot in book descriptions. Nothing could be farther from the truth.

Book descriptions are sales tools. They are basically ads, designed to get readers to buy your book. The less plot you give the reader, the better. If they know the entire plot, or big chunks of it, why should they purchase the book?

Sales are made on emotions as well as genre. The reader can be persuaded to buy in as few as three or four paragraphs. Let's look at the book description for Dean Wesley Smith's novel *The High Edge*:

"USA Today bestselling author Dean Wesley Smith returns to his fan-favorite Seeders Universe series with a fourth novel, The High Edge.

"Benny Slade lives in New York City. One moment the city around him (and everyone he knows) seems normal. The next moment, everyone dies.

"Working to survive among the dead (and plan for a future) feels impossible, but Benny doesn't give up easily. Especially when he meets the woman of his dreams, and she offers to help him and others survive.

"And then she offers him an even a bigger job, a job that could take him out into the stars."

This type of sales copy relies on name recognition or seeing the author as a bestseller. That's handled in the first paragraph along with the fact that the novel is part of a series, which might be science fiction.

The second introduces the main character, sets the scene, and gives a hint of the inciting incident that starts the action rolling.

The third gives traits of the character and entices with a promise of romance.

The fourth finishes with a plot-kicker line and reinforces the genre.

Without knowing a lot about the plot, I'm hooked.

Dean Wesley Smith is my go-to guy for advanced indie author advice. I recommend that you read his blog at http://deanwesleysmith.com and what I think is the definitive work on writing book descriptions, *How to Write Fiction Sales Copy.*

If you choose to include a brief description of your book at the beginning, make sure you put it in the file now.

3. **Determine categories and keywords.**

Choosing categories and keywords is important to getting eyes on your book. How to choose the *right* ones is a huge topic. I can't address it thoroughly in this book, but the main thing to know is that categories rely on the BISAC Subject Headings List, aka the BISAC Subject Codes List, formulated by the Book Industry Study Group http://www.bisg.org.

This list is the standard by which online retailers categorize books, based on their subject matter.

When you upload your file to your chosen online distributor or retailer, you will be offered a choice of categories to choose from, beginning with Fiction and Nonfiction. From there, the choices branch off into a multitude of genres. You get to pick two at both Amazon and Smashwords. After that, you get to pick keywords.

The main thing to know about "keywords" is that this helpful sales tool is not limited to single words. Yep, you get to use entire phrases. The retailers do restrict what you can include. For example, you can't insert your title in a keyword at Amazon, nor can you put in the names of authors of comparable books to your own. You can use terms like "sweet frontier romance 19th century america," or "mail order bride colorado homestead." Use lower case.

Amazon allows you seven keywords. Smashwords calls them "tags" and you get up to 10 of them. I say "up to ten," because there seems to be some kind of limit to length, and if you use lengthy phrases in your tags, you can't add so many. This is probably wise, due to a plethora of ridiculously long keywords and tags used by some writers in the last few years, in blatant attempts to corner the market in some genres. Don't be that writer.

4. ISBNs.

Back in Chapter 2, Section 6, I talked about International Standard Book Numbers, or ISBNs. If you have purchased your own ISBNs, you will need to use either one or two. If you are only doing an ebook version, you need one. If you will do an edition in print, you will need another. These must be different numbers.

Select the ISBNs you need from the list of numbers you purchased from Bowker. You can put the ISBN in the front matter of your ebook, if you like, but it's not required. You will want to put the ISBNs in your print book, though, on the copyright page. Some authors use both the 10- and 13-digit ISBN versions in their print books, but I believe the use of 10-digit numbers is fading. Get both versions of the number from your page at Bowker's myidentifiers site.

Later, on your release days or shortly thereafter, you will formally "assign" the ISBNs by registering them at Bowker. I remind you do take these steps in Chapters 19 and 21.

If you choose to use free ISBNs from your retailer's upload site, you must not assign or register them at Bowker.

5. Keep Going or Skip Ahead?

If you are *not* going to do a print edition of your book, skip now to Chapter 16. If you will do print, but it's not yet time to upload your ebook, you need to get other tasks related to a print edition completed, so forge ahead.

Chapter 13
PRINT BOOK FORMATTING

1. Assemble the Parts.

Back in Chapter 9, Section 1, you wrote a Configuration Master or template, detailing a uniform look and what information you will include for your books. Now you need to use that document and create the Front and Back Matter for your book. It will be similar to what you included in your ebook edition, but there are differences to keep in mind. One change is that you will not insert a book description at the front of your print book.

First, take your Final Ebook File and do a Save As, renaming it Print Interior File. Put it in the Print Book Folder

Once you have the front and back matter written, make separate files for each. This will be the same whether you are going to send your files off for formatting, or do the formatting yourself. Be sure to include the ISBN and the publisher name you are using on the copyright page. Insert the required cover design copyright or designer's name information on the copyright page.

Assemble all other elements for your print book, including any bonus material in the back, such as the first chapter of the next book, if you have that written. Save the files to the Print Book Folder

2. Templates and Guides.

CreateSpace has print format templates to download once you choose the trim dimensions for your book. These are found at

https://www.createspace.com/Help/Book/Artwork.do

You may also want to refer to other print formatting guides. I highly recommend and use a book by Heather Justesen entitled *POD Like a Pro: An Author's Guide to Typesetting and Formatting a Book for Print.* Heather's book is available in both ebook and print.

Another resource is a series of videos by Mike Petersen at KillerBookMarketing.com, who also walks you through the steps for the actual formatting. Here's the index to the series:

http://www.killerbookmarketing.com/complete-guide-formatting-createspace/

Read through the template instructions and guides and view a video or two to see if you can follow them. If not, see the remedy in the next section.

3. Contract with a Formatter

If you doubt you can do the print formatting yourself, contract with a formatter to provide the files you need. Send them the Print Interior file and the Front Matter and Back Matter files.

I have three friends who format books for print.

Maria Hoagland formats print books as well as ebooks. She offers bundle pricing for doing both formats. http://www.mariahoagland.com/formatting.html

Lindzee Armstrong formats both print books and ebooks, and offers bundle pricing. http://www.lindzeearmstrong.com/author-services/formatting-services/

Karen Hoover of Tin Bird Publications and Author Services formats for print books as well as ebooks. She also does content and line editing, and offers an extensive list of other author services. https://www.tinbirdpub.net/editing-services

Do understand that you are under no obligation to use any people I recommend in this book. I do not get a cut of any business I might send their way, so it doesn't matter to me who you make your contracts with.

4. Review the CreateSpace Process.

If you are confident you can format your book for print, first, let's review CreateSpace's process so you know what to expect and have at hand. I'm going to use "CS" to mean CreateSpace from now on. Here's what is involved:

- Start project
- Input title and author information
- Put in ISBN of your choice
- Choose the physical properties of your book: Interior Type, Paper Color—white or cream—and Trim Size.
- Upload your book interior, which must be a pdf file.
- Upload your cover, also a pdf file.
- Deal with Distribution details. Choose the cover finish—glossy or matte, add your book description, a BISAC category or code, additional information such as an author biography, Distribution Channels, and Pricing.

- Submit the files for review. CreateSpace ensures that your files meet their PDF Submission Requirements and sends you an email within 24 hours with your next steps.

Now that you know what uploading a print book will entail, let's go format yours for print.

5. Format the Print Interior file.

Format the Print Interior file in Word, or if you use InDesign, format it there. Use whatever template, guide or video best helps you.

Remember that it's more usual to have the Dedication and Acknowledgements Pages in the Front Matter of Print books than at the back.

Check that your Back Matter contains the material you want in the back of your book, such as a teaser chapter from your next book, and author notes or a biography.

Make sure you do a spell check for any errors that may have crept in. It's your last chance to get things right.

6. Save the finished file.

Do a Save As for the finished book file, putting it in your Print Book folder.

7. Save the Print final as a pdf file.

Create a pdf of your final print book file and save it in the same folder. This is the file you will upload to CreateSpace.

If you used a formatter instead of doing the work yourself, save the pdf copy he or she sends you in your folder, along with the Word or InDesign file, for your records.

The progress on your book is almost tangible enough to taste, right? You're nearly there!

Chapter 14
PRINT COVER

1. Create the Back Cover Information for Your Print Book.

In Chapter 12, Section 2, I went over some of the basics of creating sales copy disguised as a book description. The back cover of your print book can include more elements, such as an author photo and biography. However, simple is best. Don't do a cluttered look. Include your sales copy, and either bits from a couple of endorsements, or if you have a long, but particularly favorable endorsement, you may want to include it below your sales copy.

Go pull some books by your favorite authors—or authors who write in your genre—off your bookshelves and study the back covers. Note the elements of each back cover. What do you like or dislike? Make use of your research to craft a solid back cover for your book.

Be sure that if you have a logo for your publishing business, it gets included on the back cover and on the spine, if the spine is wide enough. At the very least, put your publishing imprint name (and your business website address, if you have one) on the back cover.

2. Create the Full Book Cover.

If you went the recommended route and contracted with a cover designer, this is the time to provide them with the total number of pages in your formatted book (including the front and back matter). This information allows them to create the spine of your print book at the proper thickness.

Be sure to tell them whether you are using white or cream paper at CreateSpace, as the spine measurement will be different for each.

Your cover designer will also need a copy of your back cover text and other information or images you want on the back cover. These image files will include your company logo and business website address, if any, or your author photo, if you will put a photo and biography on the back.

CreateSpace has an online cover designer tool, but using it could result in your cover looking like a hundred thousand other covers that went through the software. I do not recommend that you use it.

If you truly have the eye of a graphic artist and want to create your own book cover but don't know how to start, Derek Murphy has come up with a simple method using Word to create covers. There are other ways of course, using software programs designed to manipulate images. Here's Derek's article about how you can use Word:

http://www.creativindie.com/how-to-make-a-full-print-book-cover-in-microsoft-word-for-createspace-lulu-or-lightning-source/

You can also go to YouTube and find out how to design covers using more traditional image manipulation software programs. There are a ton of videos that will help you with this.

It's useful to include in your search terms the name of the software you will use, whether it's PhotoShop, GIMP, PowerPoint, or Paint.

Be sure to watch at least the first few minutes of each one to determine if that particular video is helpful to you. When you find a good one, watch the entire video through, remembering that you can pause at any time, or go back to review. It is most helpful if, while you watch, you do a practice cover in your chosen software.

After you create your full book cover, turn it into a pdf and save it in your Print book folder.

Chapter 15
PRINT BOOK SETUP

1. Start print setup at CreateSpace.

Back in Chapter 1, I suggested that you should set up an account at CreateSpace, found at

http://createspace.com.

If you haven't done that yet, go ahead and do it now.

From your Member Dashboard, you will start "a project," that is, work on getting a paperback edition set up for your book, so click the "Add a Title" button. The new screen is labeled "Start Your New Project." In Step 1, enter the title of your book. Be sure you spell it correctly. It says you can change it before you send it for review, but why not get it right the first time? (Okay, yes, I did misspell the title I typed in during this test run.)

Step 2 tells CS what kind of project you're doing, as CS isn't just for creating paperback books. Click the Paperback radio button (that's what the circle is called).

Step 3 gives you a choice of using the Guided setup or the Expert setup. Since this may be your first time, click the "Get Started" button on the "Guided" line. This will take you to the actual Setup part of the CS process.

(Although you won't see this right away, you may notice later that on the "Project Homepage," there are five units to each project at CreateSpace: Create, Setup, Review, Distribute, and Sales & Marketing. Each one has a "What's This?" pop-up screen with a bit more information as to what is contained inside. The pop-up for the first, Create, says "Prepare and finalize your work before getting started with the setup process." That's what you have been doing with writing your book and formatting it for print. In the Create unit, you will be urged to join the CreateSpace Community. This is a free and optional forum. It may be useful if you run into problems, but it's also a distraction at this point, as is the Preview step. I don't know of any professional writer who uses it. The other two steps are to sell you service you have already arranged for elsewhere. The second unit, Setup, is where you will actually start.)

You are now at the Title Information screen where you fill out the Title, Primary Author (that's you), and co-authors if any (who go in the "Add Contributors" section). If you don't have co-authors, don't click the Add Contributors button.

Never use ALL CAPS in your title or author information.

If your book is part of a series, here's where you add that information. If you expect your book to be part of a series, or if your book has a subtitle, you have to be careful and make sure you correlate your information with what you will put on the Kindle upload page. Section 2 has more information. Read it before you insert a subtitle or series information.

If you're not concerned about a series or a subtitle, fill in the Title and Author(s), skip the Edition number unless your book is an update of an earlier edition, change the language only if you're not publishing in English, skip the publication date, and hit the "Save and Continue" button. You may now skip Section 2 of this chapter and go to Section 3.

2. Be consistent with subtitles or series titles.

If your book has a subtitle or is part of a series, you need to be consistent in choosing the same boxes/lines you fill in when uploading the Kindle ebook and the CreateSpace print edition.

These two Amazon companies both provide a title box, a subtitle box, and a series and volume, or book number line. Be cautious what you choose when you make your series designation. Use the same areas when uploading both versions of your book.

Here's an example of how to put in a book that has a subtitle. Title: *The Hidden Sun.* Subtitle: *Essays on Grief.* No series name or volume number is needed here.

Here's an example of how to put in a series book: Title: *Spinster's Folly.* Series Name: *The Owen Family Saga.* Volume Number: 3.

If you are going to write a series of linked books, novellas, or stories without sequential volume numbers, DO use the subtitle line like this: Title: *Happy Halloween.* Subtitle: A Misty Moments Story.

You may have to notify Amazon to unite the Kindle and CreateSpace editions of your work onto one book detail page, so it helps if you're consistent and give the same information in the same areas on each upload site so the books look the same to the reader. Save time and effort, and do it right the first time.

If you have not yet done so, fill in the Title and Author(s), any subtitle or series information, then skip the Edition number unless your book is an update of an earlier edition, change the language only if you're not publishing in English, skip the publication date, and hit the "Save and Continue" button.

3. Designate an ISBN for your book.

Now you are at the ISBN screen. Every book published and distributed at CS requires an ISBN. You have three choices:

1. Use a free CS-assigned ISBN
2. Purchase a Custom Universal ISBN from CS for $99
3. Provide your own ISBN

Since I have purchased ISBNs, I use mine for print books. Your needs may differ, so you may opt to use CS's free one.

You also have the option right here of delaying your choice and skipping over this page. However, you must complete it before you can publish your book.

4. Choose the physical properties for your book.

The physical properties of your book include the Interior Type, Paper Color, and Trim Size.

The Interior Type refers to the color of the interior of your book. You will choose between Black & White or Full Color. If your book is fiction or most kinds of nonfiction, you'll want to choose Black & White. If your book has multiple color pictures or illustrations, is a children's picture book, or a graphic novel with color illustrations, you will choose Full Color.

Paper Color means do you want cream-colored paper or white paper? This is entirely up to you. I prefer cream paper for fiction, and white for nonfiction. Cream pages are said to be easier to read for long periods of time, so they're ideal for fiction. Maps and diagrams show up better on white paper. Cream paper is slightly thicker, which will affect the spine width on your full cover.

These considerations are discussed in this video from Killer Book Marketing:

https://www.youtube.com/watch?v=gmuPQjGSEow.

The final physical property you will set up is Trim Size. I've already discussed this at length in other parts of this book, so you probably already know what dimensions you will use for your book. You have the chance to choose it now.

This is as far as we will go in setting up at CS for now. Click the Save button at the bottom of the page, click on the "Return to Member Dashboard" link in the left menu to be sure your project is on the dashboard, then click "log out" up in the blue heading line where CS greets you by name.

5. Check that you are on target for your Print edition release date.

Since there is an unavoidable time component to doing a good job of proofing your print book, make sure you allow a minimum of four weeks and up to six weeks from the time you begin your work at CreateSpace to Release Day.

This involves the time you need to upload the files, get your files reviewed by CS, use the online Interior Reviewer they provide to do an initial check of the appearance of your book, order a printed proof copy, wait for the proof to arrive, and read the proof copy to find the mistakes. Allot sufficient hours or days for the proofing step. You have to read the entire book, preferably paragraph by paragraph or even sentence by sentence in reverse order (so you don't get caught up in the story). Do keep a log of where the errors are and what they are. This will assist you in the next step.

Once you have located the errors, you have to revise the text in your file to remove them, and either send the file to your print formatter for a new pdf, or reformat it as needed and make a new pdf yourself. Then upload the new file, get your files reviewed by CS, use the online Interior Reviewer again, and if all is well, hit the Publish button. If all is not well, you'll need another cycle. Allow enough time to fix errors.

Are you still on target for publishing your print book, considering the time these steps will take? Revise your print date as necessary.

Chapter 16
CREATE A BUZZ FOR YOUR EBOOK

1. Prior to release, send out your newsletter.

Now you need to make a final push to create a buzz for your book. This step can be done earlier than one week prior to Release Day, but if you have been stressed for time and haven't done anything up to now, one week is better than none.

One week before Release Day for your ebook is a good time to send out your newsletter, letting your subscribers know the exact day and date. If you have decided to lower your initial price for a week, or if you can give subscribers a Coupon Code from Smashwords for a reduced price, you let them know about your special offers. Be sure to explain that reviews are important to writers as a means of letting other people know about your subscriber's reading experience with your book, and in other ways, because the number of reviews on a book are helpful in securing future promotional slots with promoters like BookBub and Fussy Librarian.

Go ahead and ask your subscribers to leave a review for your ebook on the site where they purchased it, as well as on Amazon and on Goodreads, if they have an account there. Also encourage subscribers to tell their friends about your ebook, since word-of-mouth is still an important selling point.

2. Alert your team that your ebook release is approaching.

Now is the time to alert your fans, friends, and others—including your street team, if you have one—but at the least, those who have agreed to publicize your book, that the release is coming soon. Encourage them to tell everyone they can think of who would enjoy your book, about the approaching date. Have them use their social media contacts, just as you will, to spread the word.

3. Make use of all your social media sites to announce your forthcoming book.

Remember that Pinterest site you signed up for three years ago? Your neglected Instagram account? Or your very active Twitter stream?

Whether you have made friends and contacts on your social media places or not, go ahead and put out the word of your upcoming book on every channel you possess.

I don't mean you should spam everyone within your circle of influence, I mean you should consider being social and dropping a hint into your circles that oh yeah, you have written a book and it's coming out soon. If you have neglected the accounts, you will need to use more finesse than if you have been making friends along the way.

For example, if your book includes a dog, share a dog video on your Facebook Profile. Mention that this dog acts just like your fictional dog "Sassy," and that you hope others will enjoy the antics of the dog in your story, which will be released next Tuesday, October 3rd.

By the way, never, ever kill a dog in your book!!! Readers will not forgive you.

Go forth and do your best to let people know about your book. After all, unless *you* bring it to their attention, who else will? Err on the side of caution. Your goal isn't to overwhelm your prospective audience, but to educate them as a side comment within the context of business or common interests.

Chapter 17
UPLOAD EBOOKS
PRIOR TO RELEASE DAY

1. Upload ebook files to each online vendor.

Not surprisingly, it takes time—up to three or four days—for each online vendor to prepare and load a book detail page for your ebook. They are getting faster at it, but you must allow that time. You don't just upload your files on Release Day and wonder why nothing shows up for your readers to purchase.

If you are using a distributor that has quality controls or requires more input from you prior to their distribution (think Smashwords), you must add a few days into your timeline for uploading before your Release Day. One week beforehand is a good time allowance for distributor uploads, especially if a weekend is involved. Once you've done that, go ahead and upload to any vendors you're connecting with directly, such as Kindle Direct Publishing (KDP).

Kindle tends to get their pages up faster than others, so three to four days before release is sufficient time for the book detail page in your country's store to appear. Allow more time for International pages to generate.

To recap, if you are using a distributor instead of doing direct uploads to each vendor, allow up to a week for everything to be completed on the vendors' side. Count backwards a week from your Release Day. That's the date you upload your completed files, both ebook body and cover, to your distributor, and thereafter to each online vendor.

When uploading to KDP, as well as to all other vendors, remember the discussion on consistency in Chapter 16, Section 2. Use the guidelines within the parameters provided at each vendor. You may end up using a colon between a Title and Subtitle, or parentheses for a Series title after the main Title on the line.

2. If you use Smashwords as a distributor, download ePub and mobi files.

Once your ebook has made its way through the Meatgrinder and you have a book detail page, download the ePub and mobi files. You want to check them to make sure you or your formatter created a perfect Table of Contents.

3. Check the files on your computer.

Use the Adobe Digital Editions and Kindle Previewer software applications that I had you download in the initial stages of your book process. Adobe Digital Editions is for the ePub file, and the Kindle Previewer is for the mobi file.

If your Table of Contents links go where they are supposed to, and the external links function perfectly, you are doing great. If there are glitches, make adjustments to your files or contact your formatter for a revision, and upload to your ebook vendors again.

4. Create an Author Central account at Amazon.

An important tool at Amazon is an Author Central account. On the customer side, it's called the Amazon Author Page, but you create it at Author Central once your Kindle ebook goes live.

Here's the starting place:

https://authorcentral.amazon.com/

Amazon has good instructions for creating your account, so I won't repeat them. Do upload that Author Photo I had you take in Chapter 5.

Once you're up and running, the first task is to "claim" your ebook.

On the welcome page, under "Update your Author Page, you can add a multitude of items, but right now, you need to click on the link to "Add a book to your bibliography."

On the pop-up screen, tell Amazon the name of your book or search your author name or ISBN (if you entered one in your KDP setup). Choose your book if several appear, and it will be added to your Amazon Author Page after your name and face.

Make a note of the URL of your Amazon Author Page. You'll be giving it out to readers and using it on your website, so you may as well maintain a spreadsheet or document with these important URLs. We'll talk more about that in the next section.

5. Collect purchase links in a spreadsheet.

Very soon, your ebook is going to pop up on a lot of online vendor sites. Your task now is to track them down and make a spreadsheet (or a table in a Word document) on which you keep these vital links.

Include space for such things as the links to your website; blog, if separate; your Amazon Author Page; and profile pages at other vendors and distributors.

If you placed your ebook at the major online vendors directly or through distributors, you'll have a possibility of columns for Smashwords, Draft 2 Digital, Amazon, Barnes & Noble, Kobo, iBooks (Apple) and Google. There could be more.

Be sure to keep clean Amazon URLs, not cluttered up with anything "ref" this or that. Sharing "dirty" links from Amazon can lead to problems, such as reviews disappearing when Amazon decides you and the reviewer are related or close friends.

A typical Amazon address to give away should appear like this:

https://www.amazon.com/Zion-Trail-Promised-Valley-Book-ebook/dp/B01BJ326EY/.

I had to strip away the extra part that said "ref=1a_B003RB9P9Q_1_6?s=books&ie=UTF8&qid=1489 187344&sr=1-6". That included code only Amazon's bots understand.

Here's more information on why you must clean Amazon's links. If you give a reader a link with such extraneous words and numbers, the link can contain code pertaining to you that can sully your relationship with the reader, in Amazon's view. This could lead to a reader's review of your book being rejected, because you two are deemed to be "friends." If you give such a link to lots of people, ALL their reviews could be rejected. Always strip down Amazon links to the bare essentials before you hand them out.

Now that I've got that rant off my chest, remember that as your ebook shows up on vendor sites, gather the purchase links and enter them into your spreadsheet. Save it in a safe, intuitively retrieved place.

6. Update your sites.

Go update your website, blog, and publisher site (if you have one) with the upcoming Release Day of your ebook. If you don't yet have a page on those sites showcasing your book, add a "Books" or "My Book" page and put your book on it, complete with description, perhaps an excerpt, and most important of all, a list of purchase links, if you have them already.

I don't know how many times I've gone to look at a new author's website, and could find *no* way to buy their book, short of going to search the databases at Amazon, et. al., myself. Don't be that author!

Putting extra steps between drumming up excitement to get your book and being able to buy it is counterproductive to your sales. *Always* provide a direct link to the place or places where your readers can buy your book.

If you don't have buy links yet, be sure to update your site *after* you have them or when your book is available for purchase.

7. Add your book to online book catalogs.

Several book cataloguing and social networking sites exist on the Internet. The two best known are GoodReads and Library Thing, where readers can store and share their book catalogs and various types of book metadata. Readers can write reviews on such sites, as well.

Make sure your ebook is added to these types of databases, but be cautious about reading reviews there. Sometimes readers get carried away with emotion, and there *are* vicious people out there. Guard your tender feelings, but allow your ebook to be discoverable in as many places as possible.

Chapter 18
EBOOK RELEASE DAY

1. Announce your ebook on the designated release day.

Continue making a buzz with social media, your blog, your website, and your newsletter. Get your Street Team (if you have one) and friends in motion to share all your Facebook posts, blog posts, and Twitter tweets. Email your friends and let them know your ebook is available. Include purchase links.

Now the fun—and the tasks—begin. You may not get to all of them on Release Day, but take care of them as soon as you can.

2. Register the ebook ISBN with Bowker.

If you purchased ISBNs from Bowker, go register the one you selected to attach to your ebook.

You will need some information for your registration. I'll walk you through this.

Sign in to your account. Click the arrow beside My Account and choose Manage ISBNs.

Find the ISBN you're assigning to your book. Click Assign Title.

You're on the Title Details page, which also provided a place to upload your cover and the text of your book. Note the question mark icons alongside the boxes. These give handy information if you're unsure if the box applies to your book.

You may wish to jot down the ISBN-10, as you won't find it any other place, and sometime, somewhere, you may be asked for it. I put it on the list of ISBN numbers I received in an email when I purchased the lot. I have this paperwork in a physical file folder in a hanging file folder labeled "Publishing Essentials."

Put in your Title (and your Subtitle, if you use one). The Title is the only required box on this page, but you should fill in as much information as you can.

I'm registering the ISBN for *From Julia's Kitchen: Owen Family Cookery* as I walk you through this. *From Julia's Kitchen* is the Title. *Owen Family Cookery* is the Subtitle. This is how I put it in my KDP upload, and the print book will be the same.

You have 350 *words,* not characters, to use for your Main Description. You may wish to count these yourself, as the counter does not reduce with your input.

Original Publication Date is the year you published your book. Select the correct one.

You *do not* have to select a language. The default is English. If you are publishing your book in an additional language besides English, you will select all of them from among the choices, including English. If you're publishing in English.

If you have received a copyright on your book, select the appropriate year. The other boxes apply to special cases. If your book qualifies, give the answer requested.

Upload your cover image. Observe the minimum and maximum file sizes (4 KB min, 5 MB max). This is a good place to use the 72-dots-per-inch jpeg file, if your cover designer provided one.

Remember when I had you make a pdf file of your book text for copyright registration? Use that here to upload the "Full Text of Your Book."

Click on the "Go to: Contributors" button at the bottom of the screen.

The next page is where you enter the Contributors. This means you. The page is a bit tricky. Click on Add Contributor, then you can fill in the information in the form below. Unless you wrote your book with a co-author, you only need to fill in your first and last names, exactly as you have elsewhere, and click "Author" in the Contributor Functions. Putting in your date of birth is optional, and unless you have a very common author name, unnecessary. You may put in a biography, if you like, but it's optional, too.

Before you leave this page, notice that your name now appears in the "Contributor Name" field that appeared when you hit Add Contributor. Click on the "Go to: Format & Size" button.

There appear to be two required fields on this page: Medium, and Format. Medium is the type of book, Audio, Digital, E-Book, Packs & Multimedia, Print, Video, or Other. The Format and other fields below it will be triggered by what you choose in the Medium field.

Click on E-Book (unless you're doing this for your print book). Now your choice in Format is only Electronic book text. Select that.

Aha! Now you have another required field, Primary Subject. I'm going to choose Cooking in there, and also use the Secondary Subject to choose Fiction Historical. You go ahead and choose the most accurate description for your book in the Primary Subject field. If you need the Secondary Subject field, choose something there, too.

File Type is not a required field, and your eyes may cross at all the selections, but if you want to give this information, go ahead and choose EPUB, Kindle, or PDF, depending on how you think most of your books will be distributed. I'm going to use Kindle, although I have used EPUB in the past, as that is the other standard ebook file category.

You can go grab the File Size of your Kindle ebook from Amazon and put that in.

The rest of this page doesn't apply unless you have multiple previous editions of your book or if there is a volume number involved.

Click the "Go to: Sales & Pricing" button.

You only have a few required fields on this page. Unless the sales department of your company is very advanced, you will probably ignore many of the information fields.

When you make your initial selection of a country where your book will be sold—and you probably will choose UNITED STATES, if that is your primary market— UNITED STATES will appear in the Country Selection field, along with the flag. Other fields will change to make the adjustment, too.

Your publisher name shows up in the Publisher box.

In Title Status, choose Active Record.

In Publication Date, put in the Release Date. This is the day customers may purchase your book.

In the Target Audience, I'm going to choose Trade, as that applies to an adult audience. If you write for young adults, choose Young Adult Audience. Middle Grade authors would use Juvenile Audience. Adjust according to your book, using the fields for ages or grades, if you need to do so.

In the Currency field, choose US Dollars. In Price, put in your regular price in figures: 2.99, 4.99, 6.99, or whatever your ebook price is regularly. *Do not* use a currency symbol. In Price Type, choose Retail Price.

You may check your answers using the blue tabs to the left of the info screens. If you are finished, click SUBMIT.

You should get a pop-up screen saying your form is complete and has been saved successfully. If you don't, you may need to follow any directions given you.

You can go back at any time and adjust values that change, like if you take your book off the market (not recommended) or change your price permanently. Otherwise, you're done here, and can sign out.

3. Register the copyright to your ebook.

If you choose to obtain the extra protections of having the copyright in your book formalized by registering and paying for it, go to https://eco.copyright.gov.

This is the Electronic Copyright Office (eCO) division of the United States Copyright Office at the Library of Congress. This is where you will upload the pdf you created for this purpose.

For more information click on the help link in the upper right or use this link:

https://www.copyright.gov/eco/help/

Please note that I cannot get to the two tutorials listed upper right on this page in a usable way, as one is gobbledy-gook and the other gives an error message, but the other links work.

Once you log in to your account, you have access to circulars, and the ability to search online records. Here's a pdf on Copyright Basics:

https://www.copyright.gov/circs/circ01.pdf

This circular goes over the fees (last page) and some of the registration essentials:

https://www.copyright.gov/circs/circ04.pdf.

Note that it's quite a bit cheaper to apply for registration online ($35) than by paper application ($85).

Because the variables are many when applying for copyright registration, I won't go into more detail.

4. Update your websites again.

You may as well get used to it. Unless you are already a best-selling author with a staff of minions, you are going to do some of these tasks yourself. Make sure your websites and/or your blogs are easy to update.

Prominently display links to the online sites that carry your book for sale. *Don't be coy and embed the links within the text of your showcase page.* The links can be easily overlooked. I swore up and down to one new author that she didn't have any purchase links on her website. She insisted that she did. I found them finally. There they were in the text of the page, but the links were almost invisible due to the color scheme she had chosen for the text and background, and the fact that she arranged for links not to be underlined! (Yes, some sites allow that. No, you should not do it.)

Use buttons or a clearly labeled area with all the places your book is for sale. If you use Amazon KDP Select, make sure Amazon is in bold letters, with the link attached to the word. If you chose wide distribution, do an array of the retailers, maybe separated by the "pipe" symbol. Mine is above my enter key next to brackets, as the Shift character above the backfacing slash \. The pipe symbol looks like this | and it's a handy separator between vendors:

Kindle | NOOK | Kobo | iBooks | Smashwords

Anyway, do update your website or sites to reflect the current availability of your book.

5. Submit materials to online publicity sites of published books.

As my checklist has evolved, I've written notes in the margins of my printouts, reminding myself to inform various places that my book is live and for sale. You may have identified such sites yourself.

Because my religion is LDS (I'm a Mormon), which is a niche market, but an active one, I like to keep one site run by an LDS woman updated about my new novels. The site is called New LDS Fiction, which is a showcase for fiction written by LDS authors. It's found at http://www.newldsfiction.com/. There's a form to fill out to submit book information. The proprietor adds books to her website as they come in. In addition, each Saturday she sends an email to her subscribers detailing the new books that were published that week.

I also upload my new books to a site called My Book Ratings found at https://mybookratings.com/, which allows me to content-rate my books so readers know what is coming at them before they buy.

You have probably run across other sites where readers can discover your books. Make sure you take the time to submit your book information in this crucial post-release time frame.

6. Inform your writers' organizations.

Many organizations for writers have a periodic newsletter or blog, and publicize new books published by members.

Get familiar with the announcement parameters for your

associations. Send information and purchase links (if they'll take them) to your groups to take advantage of this benefit. Include your cover image, your bio, and possibly your author photo. Depending on if your group publishes on the web or in print, send the correct sort of image files: a 2-inch by 3-inch headshot of your author photo in 300 dpi for print, and 72 dpi for blogs or websites, reduced to a web-friendly file size. Do send similar files for your cover, no more than 400 pixels by 600 pixels in width/height dimensions.

7. Open an account at Authorgraph and add your ebook.

Have you avoided doing ebooks because you can't, you know, sign them? Look back to Chapter 5, and refresh your memory about Authorgraph. Now go open your account at http://www.authorgraph.com/ and add your book. Grab the widget if you want it on your website or blog, to let readers know you *can* sign their ebook.

8. Open accounts of your choice for book sales tracking.

Back in Chapter 3, I discussed book tracking services. If you decided to pay for book sales tracking, open an account at BookTrakr or another site of your choice. Add or claim your book.

9. Carry out marketing efforts of your choice.

Marketing is beyond the scope of this book. You will find numerous discussions on the Internet, in Facebook Groups, and in books about what is current and working. "What is working" is important, because that always seems to change as the New Best Idea comes along.

However some marketing principles never change, so educate yourself.

Ask in your writers groups what the members do for their marketing efforts. Tell them you want them to be honest about results. Good luck!

Chapter 19
FOUR TO SIX WEEKS BEFORE
PRINT BOOK RELEASE DAY

1. Gather print book interior and book cover files.

By now, you should have received both the print book file from your formatter, plus the full cover you contracted for from your cover designer. Alternately, if you created these files, you have them safely tucked away in the proper folder.

These will be pdf files. Locate them now, because it's time to upload them at CreateSpace.

2. Upload both Print Book pdf and Cover pdf to CreateSpace.

Go to the Internet and log into your CreateSpace account at

https://www.createspace.com/.

From your Member Dashboard, click on the title of your book to bring up the Project Homepage. Under Setup, click on Interior.

Find the box alongside "PDF Interior File" (which has a red "required" asterisk beside it). Click the Browse button to find the pdf of your Print Interior File on your computer. Since you're probably uploading a novel, make sure the default radio button (circle) beside Bleed says "Ends **before** the edge of the page." Follow the directions to upload the file, and wait until it is accepted.

Now upload the PDF of your full cover by clicking the "PDF Cover File" circle and browsing for the file. Wait until that is accepted, as well.

3. Finish Setup at CreateSpace.

Before you can submit your interior and cover files for review, you need to finish a few steps of setup. These include Description, Channels, and Pricing, which all fall under the Distribution Unit of CS.

The description tells potential customers about your book. It's the major sales copy, and you probably used it on the back cover of your book, too. The description you put in the box displays in your eStore and on your book's Amazon.com detail page, and may be used as your book's description in other sales channels you choose. The description can have up to 4,000 characters, or about 760 words.

You probably sweated long and hard over the description back in Chapter 12. Put it in the box now.

You only get one BISAC category at CS, so make sure it's the best one for your book that is also a top-tier category. Choose Fantasy, in other words, and use the keywords down below to drill down into the subgenres of Fantasy to get to Shapeshifting Turtles.

Add an author bio if you want.

If you're publishing in English, leave the language box as is. Choose the Country of Publication. It's probably the United States, right?

Now for keywords. You worked on these in Chapter 12, as well. At CreateSpace, you get up to about 25 characters for each one, up to five of them, each separated by a comma and a space. There may be more than one word inside the keyword. For example, you may want to use "mail order brides for Louisiana alligator hunters" as a keyword. However, that exceeds the 25-character limit, so you would have to break it up.

If you've written a racy book, you'll have to tick off the "Contains Adult Content" checkbox. Click the What's this? link for more information.

"Large print" is designated for books of 16-point text or larger aimed at the eyesight-impaired population.

Continue on and choose the distribution channels that will best serve you. You can come back later to set up your eStore and any Discount Codes you wish to offer.

Now determine what price you want to charge for your book.

When you have finished all the steps to complete the setup, click on the "Submit for Review" button at the bottom of the page. Your files are going to be checked, so there's nothing more to do here. Go ahead and log out. Resist any suggestion that you let CS publish your book on Kindle for you. You will do a better job yourself.

Your files will be checked within the next 24 hours to ensure your setup information is correct and your files are printable. You will be e-mailed the result once your review is complete.

If you have errors, CS will tell you that, and you can remedy them. If the files are fine, go on to the next step.

4. Check your book for visual errors.

CS offers you a choice of ways to review the looks of your book file. You may use the nifty online Interior Reviewer, download a pdf to view on your computer or device, or order a printed proof copy to be sent to you. I would advise you to use all three methods.

Go through the online Reviewer a number of times, as they suggest, looking at different aspects of the book each time: format, images, and grammatical errors or typos.

Download the pdf to check for the same type of errors offline.

Order a proof copy. You will pay for the printing cost and the shipping, and it is well worth the price to have the printed book in your hands. That way, you can physically judge if the margins are correct and if the colors of the cover look as you imagine they should. Matte covers usually print darker than glossy ones do, in case you need to make an adjustment there.

5. Allow up to two weeks for proof to arrive.

It's going to take a while for your proof copy to arrive. It may take up to two weeks, although it usually doesn't take that long. In the meantime, go take care of something on the ebook release follow-up list in Chapter 18 that you haven't finished.

6. Check the print proof copy.

This may take several days, as I explained back in Chapter 15.

Do take the time to find the errors and fix anything glaring. It's easy to fix an ebook file, but there's something daunting about uploading a third or fourth print pdf, so make it your best work on this pass.

As I suggested, read your book backwards so you don't get caught up in the story. Go paragraph by paragraph, or even sentence by sentence if yours are long and convoluted.

If you used a wrong, but correctly-spelled word, which spell check couldn't possible find, you will discover it using this method.

As I suggested previously, make an error log, noting where the errors occur on the printed page: chapter by chapter, scene by scene, page by page, and paragraph by paragraph (number them from the top of the page down). They won't be found in the manuscript copy in the same place, but they will in the formatted-for-print copy, which you will copy to a new filename and then correct. You will also need to make corrections to your manuscript copy so if anything is wrong in the ebook, it can be corrected ASAP. Do try for consistency among the versions you have available to your readers. The error log will help you find and change the mistakes.

When you have corrected the formatted file, make a new pdf and upload it. Now you will submit it again for review, and then check it again after CS clears it. It's probably not necessary to order another printed proof, although some people just *must* do so.

See why I told you four to six weeks might be required?

When you have no errors, go to CS for the next step.

7. Approve the proof. Publish your book.

Go back and log in at CreateSpace. Go to your Project Homepage. Under Review, there's probably an "Action Required" icon next to "Proof Your Book." Click the link.

No matter how many times you've uploaded a new file, the time comes to get on with publishing your book. Everything is perfect, right?

Scroll down, take a deep breath, and click on the button reading "Approve Book Proof."

This will "publish" your book, and Amazon's minions will immediately begin compiling your book detail page. We hope they encounter the one for your ebook and the information matches up so exactly that they only need to add the print book details to the existing page. (This may or may not happen. You may need to contact Amazon to get a unified book detail page.)

Hurrah! Your book is published!

Maybe it isn't "released" yet, as in "I have a big Release Day Party planned," but it will be available for purchase in print shortly. Usually within 24 hours on the Amazon US page.

So you're done, right?

Wrong. See the next section.

8. Order print book copies.

I know it will be tempting to order a gazillion copies of your print book. Hold on, Skippy! Times have changed. You are most likely not going to need a huge bunch of printed copies. They will cost you upfront money, and you will have to store them, so listen up: order only the amount of copies you expect to sell in the next three months.

If you have a big Book Release Party planned for launch day, with confirmed attendees who are sure to buy the book, go ahead and order that amount of copies plus 3-5 extras. All Good Luck to you in selling out your inventory! Send any who didn't show up on time to buy a book to Amazon or Barnes and Noble.com, and promise to autograph their books when they come.

If you have a large support community surrounding you, and you know you're going to move 50 copies of the printed book in the next three months, order 55 copies. If you took pre-orders for the books and you *know* you have pre-sold that number, that's even better.

If you're going to a writers' conference with a bookstore or a book signing for attendees, order 15 copies. I know. That's far fewer than you think you should sell, but if this is your first book, please be realistic. If nobody has heard of you, unless you've been doing a bang-up job of promoting your book, you're not going to move a lot of copies to other writers, and the book signings only draw readers of the mega-authors in attendance. Think of the wear and tear you will avoid to the books and your body in getting fewer books there, carting them around, and getting them home.

Yeah, I know. This doesn't sound optimistic at all. However, your main goal for doing print copies should be to have a *few* on hand for those diehards who won't buy your ebooks.

When your stock in hand dips below five and you have a writers' event coming up, go ahead and re-order another five.

For the love of all you hold dear, *do not* order 300 copies of your precious book mumblemumble like I did with my first bookmumblemumble. Times have changed. You don't want that many books a-moldering in your basement or garage, taking ten years to sell. Print-on-Demand is awesome. Only print the number of books you need to fulfill an actual demand!

9. Wait for copies to arrive.

There is an eternal wait between the time you order your first real print copies and the time they arrive. Fortunately, time moves faster on the Amazon website and you have plenty of chores to take care of. You must finish up plans for your book release, if you're doing a grand hard release, with a party, either physical or online. Enlist your fellow authors to help you do a Facebook Release Party. Or cajole a local independent bookstore into hosting your Release Party, and bring cookies and candy to celebrate. Or have a bonfire party in your back yard, or release your book at a riding stable, or somewhere related to the subject of your book. A bakery? A tux shop? KFC? There's no end of possibilities.

Take care of a couple of other chores:

10. Claim print book at Author Central when it appears.

Instead of haunting the front porch or the mailbox, check your book detail page a couple of times a day until you see your print copy appear. When it does, go to your Amazon Author Central account and "claim" the book as your own.

On the Welcome page, find "Add a book to your bibliography" click the link, and follow the directions.

11. Make sure ebook and print book are linked on Amazon.

Both book editions should appear on the same book detail page within about 24 hours.

If, horror of horrors, you look in vain for your print book to show up on the existing ebook page at Amazon, you do a search, and *there is a separate page*, you might have made some teensy little error when you put in your book title information. Or not.

If this happens to your book, you need to click the help link on your Author Central page. It's up there beside your name. You can elect to have a representative call you. I like this option, in case my situation is complex, but a simple email may do the trick for you. Whatever the contact you choose, don't panic. Most boo-boos can be worked out quite quickly, and with a minimum of tears.

Chapter 20
PRINT BOOK RELEASE DAY

1. Announce the print book launch on the designated day.

O frabjous day! Callooh, Callay! It's Release Day, and you're having a big to-do.

You planned it all beforehand, and now the big day is here. If you're doing a physical release day event, don't neglect the online crowd. Make sure your helpers are tweeting, posting, blogging, and generally raising a ruckus about your book. Make sure your website is up-to-date. Today is the day to buzz the daylights out of your wonderful creation!

2. Add the print edition to GoodReads.

If you haven't done so already, get the print edition linked to the ebook edition. You may need to find a GoodReads Librarian to combine the editions for you, but just ask on Facebook, and they'll pop out of the woodwork.

3. Register the print ISBN with Bowker.

Go back and take care of your second ISBN, if you chose to purchase them. Do essentially the same thing as in Chapter 18, Section 2.

4. Carry out the marketing efforts of your choice.

I'm not getting into marketing in this book. I don't know if I ever will write a book on marketing, because it's such a "new-best-thing" area of endeavor.

Look around. Ask around. Choose one thing to try that won't suck up all your energy, money and time. After all, you have another book to write, yes?

Take a little time to bask in your truly great accomplishment, but not too much time. You have another book to write. I'll repeat that again: you have another book to write. Nothing sells your first book better than having a second book available.

But for now, you've completed your goal, and thus, my work is done.

It's been a pleasure to work with you. I hope I was of some help and comfort along the way in getting your book prepared and out to market. Enjoy the feeling of accomplishing something that millions of other people wish they could do, but don't have the drive and ambition to manage.

Have a wonderful day!

Thank You!

Please post a review of this book on your favorite review or purchase site. Reviews from readers, even as few as twenty words, make all the difference to those browsing and buying books.

Remember to recommend this book to your writer friends, telling them how helpful it is to you. Word-of-mouth recommendations are valuable rewards for authors.

Subscribe to Marsha Ward's Readers Club to receive advance notice of coming book releases. http://eepurl.com/vBKEj

About the Author

Best-selling author Marsha Ward writes authentic historical fiction set in 19th Century America, contemporary romance, and nonfiction. She was born in the sleepy little town of Phoenix, Arizona, in a simpler time. With plenty of room to roam among the chickens and citrus trees, Marsha enjoyed playing with neighborhood chums, but always had her imaginary friend, cowboy Johnny Rigger Prescott, at her side.

Now she makes her home in a forest in the mountains of Arizona. She loves to hear from her readers.

Connect with her at:

Website: marshaward.com
Blog: marshaward.blogspot.com
Email: marshaw@marshaward.com
Facebook: www.facebook.com/authormarshaward
Twitter: twitter.com/MarshaWard